AN OXBRIDGE WALK

Leighton Lock, Grand Union Canal (Buckinghamshire)

AN OXBRIDGE WALK

by

JAMES A. LYONS

Line illustrations and country route maps
by John Johnson

CICERONE PRESS
MILNTHORPE, CUMBRIA

© James A. Lyons 1995
ISBN 1 85284 166 4
A catalogue record for this book is available from the British Library

DEDICATION
For Foz and the lads

I will make a traveller of thee
If ruled by this book thou wilt be.

John Bunyan (Apology from *Pilgrim's Progress*)

Front Cover: Radcliffe Camera

CONTENTS

INTRODUCTION 7

ROUTES

Oxfordshire: 17
    Oxford to Great Milton 19
    Great Milton to Thame 28

Buckinghamshire: 34
    Thame to Cuddington 35
    Cuddington to Quainton 42
    Quainton to Swanbourne 51
    Swanbourne to Leighton Buzzard 56

Bedfordshire: 64
    Leighton Buzzard to Woburn 66
    Woburn to Ampthill 74
    Ampthill to Clophill 83
    Clophill to Northill 93
    Northill to Gamlingay 104

Cambridgeshire: 113
    Gamlingay to Arrington (Wimpole Hall) 114
    Wimpole Hall to Cambridge 122

Alternative Route - Oxfordshire/Buckinghamshire 132
    Oxford to Pigeon Lock 134
    Pigeon Lock to Stratton Audley 144
    Stratton Audley to Hillesden 151
    Hillesden to Swanbourne 155

APPENDIX 162

    Way-marked, middle/long-distance footpaths in the
    four counties 162

    Some Useful Addresses 165

ACKNOWLEDGEMENTS

Sally drew the section maps, took the colour photographs, compiled the accommodation lists and, often literally, 'went the extra mile' that made the book possible.

Many thanks are also due to John Murray (Publishers) Ltd for permission to quote from the *Collected Works of John Betjeman*.

In addition, I am endebted to the following people and organisations for their help and advice: Hugh Potter and Shanie Holbrow, Countryside Service, Oxfordshire County Council; Mike Furness, County Engineers Dept, Bucks County Council; Peter Currell, Aylesbury Vale District Council; Julian Scot, Bucks County Museum; Phil Marsh, Bucks Railway Centre; Ken Reading, local historian, Bucks; Andy Turner, County Leisure Services; Stephen Coleman, Planning and Records Office, Bedfordshire County Council; The Shuttleworth Collection; Alan Bigg, local historian, Beds; Richard Dales, Rural Group, Cambridgeshire County Council.

Gill Green, who walked and assisted on sections in each county, and last, but not least Saddam Hussein.

ADVICE TO READERS

Readers are advised that whilst every effort is taken by the author to ensure the accuracy of this guidebook, changes can occur which may affect the contents. A book of this nature with detailed descriptions and detailed maps is more prone to change than a more general guide. New fences and stiles appear, way-marking alters, there may be new buildings or eradication of old buildings. It is advisable to check locally on transport, accommodation, shops etc. Even rights-of-way can be altered, paths can be eradicated by landslip, forest clearances or changes of ownership. The publisher would welcome notes of any such changes.

INTRODUCTION

The walk is about 115 miles long between the cities of Oxford and Cambridge, thereby linking the two most prestigious universities in the country, if not the world. In order to achieve this it traverses four counties and a surprisingly varied landscape along rights-of-way which deserve to be more widely used and better known. The route, therefore, opens new horizons in that it provides a fairly direct cross-country route using less familiar footpaths across the secret heart of England.

The whole walk could be completed in a week but to do it full justice requires at least two weeks since there are a number of worthwhile visits and detours en route. In fact, the basis of organisation is flexible enough for it to be tailored to suit most requirements since it is arranged in short sections averaging around 10 miles. It could, for instance, be completed by breaking it down into sections which could be walked separately over a much longer period, or the visits and detours could be used as the basis for one-day walking excursions. However, for maximum effect the Oxbridge Walk is best tackled as a single enterprise, although whether it should be walked starting at Oxford or Cambridge is really only a matter of preference since it works equally well in either direction.

The route heads in a generally north-easterly direction across the four counties of Oxfordshire, Buckinghamshire, Bedfordshire and Cambridgeshire. Where possible it incorporates all or part of way-marked middle- and long-distance paths which provide an easily followed route. At both the Oxford and Cambridge ends such footpaths either do not exist or are not suited to the requirements of the Oxbridge route. Therefore, a route has been devised that is fairly direct and which incorporates a high level of interest across an attractive landscape. Sketch maps have been provided at the start of each section which should enable the route to be easily followed, whilst the general information at the end of each section includes any available bed-and-breakfast and/or camping accommodation. Oxfordshire is not a particularly large county, since it is only 50 miles at its longest with a maximum width of 33 miles, and the whole county lies within the basin of the Thames and its tributaries.

AN OXBRIDGE WALK

OXFORD

OXFORD · M40 · THAME · A41 · LEIGHTON BUZZARD · A5 · M1

INTRODUCTION

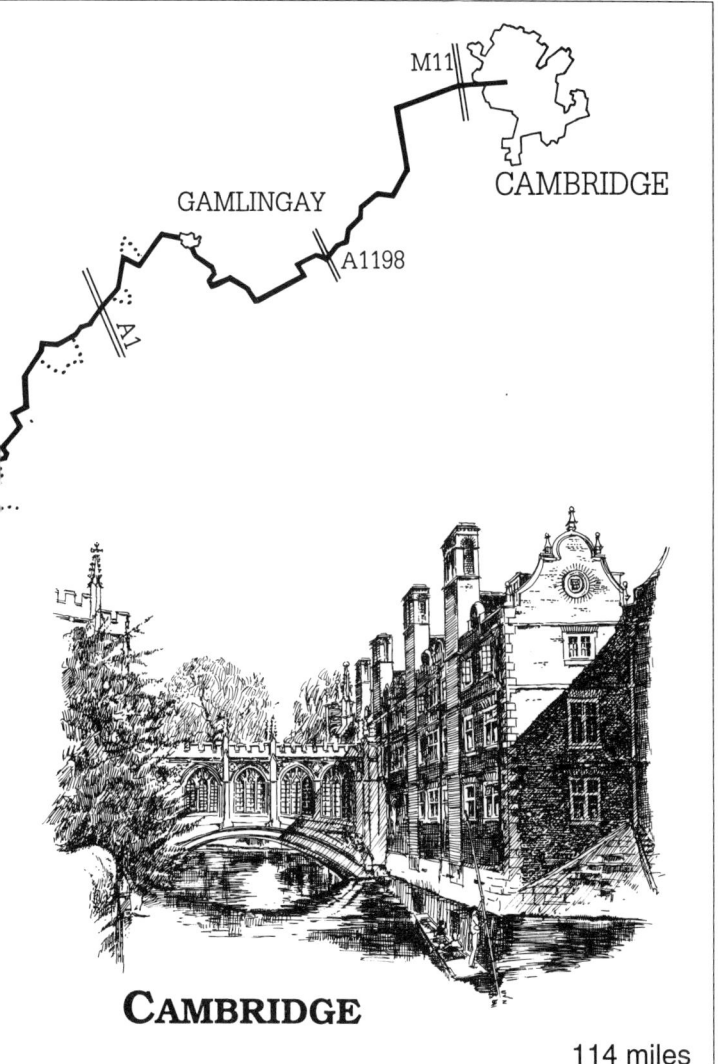

CAMBRIDGE

114 miles

However, within its 750 square miles it has much to offer, sandwiched as it is between the two well-known walking areas of the Cotswolds and the Chilterns.

Two routes are on offer out of Oxford at this end of the Oxbridge Walk. The northerly route leaves the city via the Oxford Canal, on a route which rejoins the main walk in Buckinghamshire (described in detail in the appendix). The main, southerly route begins by following the River Thames south for 3 miles. This is a particularly interesting stretch of the river, being the focus of university rowing activities and at the same time a haven for wildlife. The route leaves the Thames and travels east over mainly pastoral farmland which could not be described as hilly but which, once clear of the Thames valley, is rarely flat. The route includes the hill-top villages of Garsington and Cuddesdon from which there are good all-round views of the surrounding countryside, whilst Great Milton and Great Haseley are attractive examples of the type of Oxfordshire village which has made the county so popular with tourists.

The route through Oxfordshire has been divided into the following easily walked sections:

Oxford to Great Milton	9 miles
Great Milton to Thame	9 miles

Way-marking: Standard public footpath/bridleway signposts and arrows. In the absence of existing middle-distance link-paths from the centre of the city, a route has been devised which is fairly direct and easy to follow. The route across Oxfordshire begins by following the Thames Walk for 3 miles downstream. Thereafter, the usual metal finger-posts indicate where the right-of-way leaves the public highway; bridle tracks are marked with blue arrows and footpaths with yellow.

Ordnance Survey Maps:

1:50,000 Landranger No.164 Oxford & surrounding area

1:25,000 Pathfinder No.1116 Oxford (SP 40/50)

1:25,000 Pathfinder No 1117 Thame (SP 60/70)

Comments on way-marking and the condition of the paths should be addressed to:- Dept of Leisure and Arts, Countryside

Service, Holton, Oxford OX33 1QQ. (01865) 810226.

Buckinghamshire is another relatively small county, being only 50 miles from north to south and generally less than 20 miles wide. It is primarily an agricultural county but, in spite of its size, offers good walking. The Oxbridge route continues in a generally west-to-east direction and incorporates paths, some fairly recently opened, which explore some of the less widely known and appreciated areas in the county.

The route first follows the new Thame Valley Walk from Thame as far as Eythrope Park. The Kimmeridge clay of the Thame Valley bottom provides wetlands and damp pastures, ditches and ponds, and the River Thame is a refuge for some less common forms of wildlife. A range of wild flowers manages to survive in the hedgerows and along the margins of the intensively cultivated fields and the Thame Valley is one of the very few areas in Buckinghamshire where fritillaries have been found. At Eythrope Park the route picks up the Swan's Way and the North Bucks Way/Midshires Way as they head north out of the Thame Valley and, eventually, over Quainton Hill. This hill, one of the outcrops of Portland and Purbeck limestones which account for the hills in this area of the county, is the highest point on the Oxbridge Walk and provides panoramic views over the surrounding countryside. On the other side of Quainton Hill, the route stays with the Swan's Way as far as Swanbourne where it picks up the Cross Bucks Way to run east across gently undulating farmland to complete the west-east crossing of the county at Leighton Buzzard.

The route across Buckinghamshire has been divided into the following easily walked sections:-

Thame to Cuddington	7 miles
Cuddington to Quainton	9 miles
Quainton to Swanbourne	8 miles
Swanbourne to Leighton Buzzard	9 miles

Way-marking: Long-distance footpaths/bridleway markings as follows -

Thame Valley Walk   Metal finger posts, plastic discs

North Bucks Way	Metal finger posts, plastic discs
Cross Bucks Way	Metal finger posts, plastic discs.
Swan's Bridleway	Plastic discs with swan's head and horseshoe emblem.
Midshires Way	Plastic discs with double acorn logo.

Ordnance Survey Maps:

1:50,000 Landranger	165 (Aylesbury and Leighton Buzzard Area)
1.25,000 Pathfinder	1117 (SP 60/70) Thame
	1093 (SP 61/71) Ambrosden and Waddesdon
	1070 (SP 62/72) Winslow and Stratton Audley
	1071 (SP 82/92) Leighton Buzzard and Stewkley

Comments on way-marking and condition of the above paths should be addressed to:- Rights-of-Way Officer, County Engineer's Dept, County Hall, Aylesbury HP20 1UY. (01296) 382171.

Bedfordshire has the longest single footpath, the Greensand Ridge Walk, of the Oxbridge route. In places it also provides a contrast with the route through the other calcareous counties since it provides growing conditions suitable for acid loving plants and a habitat which attracts a different range of wildlife. As it traverses the county for 43 miles from west to east, the route incorporates detours and visits to a surprising number of places of interest deserving of appreciation by a wider public. Not for nothing, in this context, has Bedfordshire been called the secret county.

The path roughly follows the Greensand Ridge which is cut through by two river valleys, the Ouzel, almost at the start of the walk, and the Ivel, almost at the end. The ridge is generally 4 or 5 miles wide and where it outcrops in the form of hard sandstone it forms a ridge which can be easily seen and followed and is good walking, since it is sandy and free-draining. It also provides a refuge for what remains of the heather, gorse and broom which once covered its entire length and habitat for the birds and insects that thrive in open, sandy places.

The Greensand, however, does not exist as a single, continuous ridge, as it is overlaid in places by a cap of chalky, boulder clay.

These stretches can make for muddy walking conditions but have the compensation of diversifying the habitat and thereby the wildlife, especially in areas where the sand and the clay meet, such as in Maulden Wood. In the past such areas of heavy clay were often left as woodland, and remnants of ancient woods still survive along the line of the ridge and are important for many of the county's more interesting bird and animal species. All three woodpeckers are to be found, nuthatches, tree pipits, woodcocks and pheasants; and, more rarely, redstarts and woodwarblers. In addition, it is not uncommon to sight deer, especially the muntjac, originally escapees from the deer park at Woburn.

The Greensand Ridge Walk is divided into the following easily walked sections:-

Leighton Buzzard to Woburn	8 miles
Woburn to Ampthill	11 miles
Ampthill to Clophill	7 miles
Clophill to Northill	8 miles
Northill to Gamlingay(Cambs)	9 miles

Way-marking - Muntjac deer emblem on metal finger-posts; plastic discs and branded, (GRW) oak-posts in some areas of open country, parkland, woods, etc.

Ordnance Survey Maps:

1:50,000 Landranger 165 (Aylesbury and Leighton Buzzard)
                    153 (Bedford and Huntingdon)
1:25,000 Pathfinder SP 93 (Woburn)
                    TL 15 (St Neots South)
                    SP 82/92 (Leighton Buzzard and Stewkley)
                    TL 03/13 (Hitchin North and Ampthill)
                    TL 04/14 (Bedford South and Biggleswade)
                    TL 25/35 (Gamlingay and Comberton)

Comments on way-marking and the condition of the path should be addressed to:- Access and Development Officer, Leisure Services Dept., County Hall, Bedford MK42 9AP (01234) 228336.
Cambridgeshire is generally thought of as a flat county, best known for its fens, but it does have upland areas on the "shores" of what,

before drainage, was virtually an inland sea for much of the year. The final stretch of the Oxbridge route takes full advantage of the upland area known as the Cambridgeshire Heights to create a walk which is a fitting end to the journey from Oxford to Cambridge. The first half of the route follows the recently created Clopton Way across low upland farming areas of chalky boulder clay. Here the prairie-like fields of cereal crops denuded of hedgelines contrast with the generally smaller scale farming in previous counties. Wildlife survives in spite of intensive cultivation although it is only to be found in abundance in oases such as Potton Wood - an SSSI incorporated in the route. Later it follows the line of an escarpment which, although only a few hundred feet high, gives outstanding views across the surrounding flat countryside. Wimpole Hall, the most spectacular house in Cambridgeshire, marks the end of the Clopton Way and a memorable mid-way point on this last stretch of the Oxbridge Walk. After Wimpole Hall, the route follows bridle-tracks up and over a last hill to give the first, distant view of Cambridge across the broad main valley of the Cam, with the line of radio telescopes clearly visible in the middle distance. From here the route lies down into the valley through the Eversdens and the line of radio telescopes to eventually join the Wimpole Way for the last few miles into Cambridge.

The Oxbridge route started at a bridge over the Thames in Oxford and, after crossing over the Cambridge Backs, it ends at a bridge over the Cam. The 115-mile journey between the two most famous university cities in the country is over, but with Cambridge still to explore it could be said that the adventure has only just begun.

The route through Cambridgeshire is divided into the following easily walked sections:-

Gamlingay to Arrington (Wimpole Hall)   9 miles
Arrington to Cambridge   11 miles

Way-marking - The Clopton Way and the Wimpole Way are marked by metal finger-posts and circular, plastic discs. The section of the route after Wimpole Hall follows standard way-marking for public footpaths and bridleways.

Ordnance Survey Maps:

1:50,000 Landranger	No.153 Bedford, Huntingdon and surrounding area
	No.154 Cambridge, Newmarket and surrounding area
1:25,000 Pathfinder	1003 TL25/35 Gamlingay and Comberton

Comments on way-marking and the condition of the paths should be addressed to:- Rights-of-Way Officer, Rural Management Division, Dept of Property, Cambridge CB3 OAP. (01223) 317404.

Millions of tourists visit Oxford and Cambridge each year and hundreds of guides have been written which do justice to the two most important touristic cities in England outside of the capital, London. The following basic information will prove useful as a starting point for those proposing to visit the cities and/or undertake the Oxbridge Walk.

OXFORD

Tourist information	St Aldates, (nr Christchurch), Oxford OX1 1DY (01865) 726871
B+B accommodation	Book a Bed (as above)
	YHA Jack Straw's Lane, Oxford OX3 ODW (01865) 62997
Camping	Oxford International & shop (01865) 246551
	Salter's Boatyard, Donnington Bridge (01865) 243421
Outdoor shops	YHA shop, 9-10 St Clements (01865) 247948
	Millets, 42/43 Queen St (01865) 790676
Access	Road (M40)
	Four park & ride car parks
	Rail (Oxford Station) (01865) 722333
	Bus (01865) 711312
	Coach (01865) 791579
	(Varsity Link) (01223) 236333
	(Heathrow/Gatwick) (01865) 722270

CAMBRIDGE

Tourist information	Wheeler St, Cambridge CB2 3QB (01223) 322640
B+B accommodation	Book a Bed (as above)
	YHA 97 Tenison Rd, Cambridge CB1 2DN (01223) 354601
Camping (nearest)	Highfield Farm Camping Park, Long Road, Combe (4 miles SW on Oxbridge route) (01223) 262308
Outdoor shops	Blacks Camping & Leisure, Regent St. (01223) 314335
	Army & Navy Stores, St Andrews St. (01223) 357620
	Millets, 26 St Andrews St. (01223) 352169
	YHA, 6 Bridge St. (01223) 353956
	Open Air, 11 Green St. (01223) 324666
Access	Road M11 (2 park & ride car parks)
	Rail Cambridge Station (01223) 311999
	Bus (01223) 423554 or (01480) 463792
	Coach (01223) 460711
	(Varsity/Airport Link) (01223) 236333

OXFORDSHIRE
OXFORD - THAME

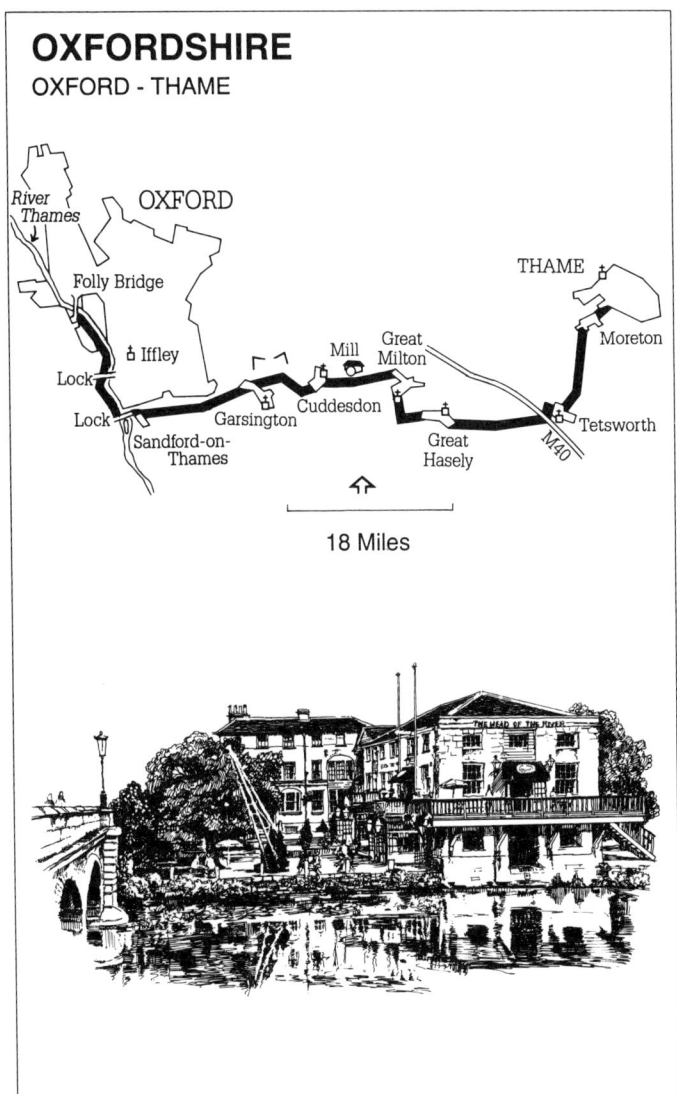

AN OXBRIDGE WALK

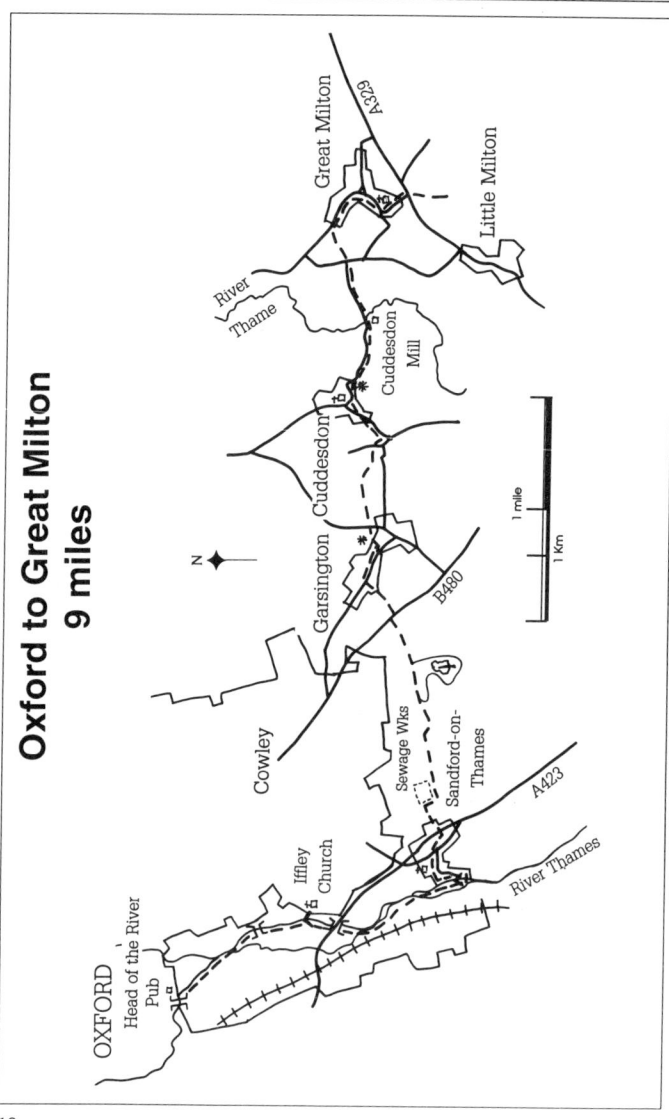

Oxford to Thame: 18 miles

OXFORD - IFFLEY LOCK - GARSINGTON - CUDDESDON - GREAT MILTON - (9 miles)

Of particular interest

City of Oxford and University Colleges; Start of Oxbridge Walk - Head of the River pub, Folly Bridge; River Thames; Iffley - Norman church, lock; Sandford on Thames - lock; Garsington - viewpoint; Cuddesdon - Theological College, Water-mill; Great Milton church, Great House, restaurant.

At the bottom of St Aldate's (a corruption of "Old Gate") is Folly Bridge over the River Thames. On the same side of the road as Christ Church, and this side of the river, stands the well-known Head of the River pub, where the Oxbridge Walk begins its journey of over 100 miles to Cambridge.

This pub is, in fact, a converted grain warehouse and offers splendid views of passing river traffic from its second floor balcony overlooking the Thames. The pub has boating memorabilia and photographs on display relating to the boat races held on the river (also known as the Isis) below Folly Bridge. Eights Week, in late May, almost rivals Henley Royal Regatta as a social occasion and is as keenly contested as the annual Oxford/Cambridge boat race. The winning eight receives a cup for their efforts and for that year reign as Head of the River.

From the pub the route crosses over Folly Bridge, past the Salter Bros booking office, and turns left down a flight of stone steps to the path along the river bank.

A memorable start to the journey could be made by booking a one-way ticket on the passenger river-boat which runs downstream several times a day from here - Salter Bros booking office: (01865) 243421/2.

The route, for those who prefer to begin the way they mean to carry on, follows the river-bank path downstream on the right-hand side of the river for the next 3 miles.

The path below Folly Bridge passes college sports fields on the right and a last sight of Oxford's 'dreaming spires' across Christ Church meadow on the opposite bank.

This is a particularly interesting stretch of the river since it is where college rowing activities are concentrated throughout the year, and eights crews are coached from dawn till dusk in preparation for the big day.

A row of college boat houses is soon passed on the opposite side of the river just below which is the confluence of the Thames and Cherwell, whilst on this side of the river the path crosses a footbridge and runs past the front of the Oxford University Boat Club.

Further along, another boat house is passed and two footbridges are crossed separated by an area designated Longbridge's Nature Park, run by Oxford City Council. Below here, the path continues under Donnington Bridge on the other side of which, on the opposite bank, is Salter's Boat Yard.

This boat yard is combined with a small campsite. Those looking for more luxurious camping facilities should take the footpath on the right, about 50 yards below the bridge. Here a wooden swing gate, next to a red and white metal pole, gives access to a path which will take them close to Oxford's biggest and best known campsite, Oxford Camping International. This is a five-star campsite immediately opposite a park-and-ride car park, with a bus service into the city every 15min.

Below Donnington Bridge as far as the next road bridge (A423 ring road), the path follows the river-bank with Iffley Meadows, an SSSI managed by the Berkshire, Buckinghamshire and Oxfordshire Naturalists' Trust (BBONT), on the right.

Iffley Meadows is accessible to the public and consists of 82 acres of ancient wet meadowland, one of the few places remaining in Britain where fritillaries flower in their natural surroundings. The meadows are managed traditionally and are only mown in July after the seed from the fritillary plants has ripened. Apart from fritillaries they carry a wide variety of plants, many of which are indicators of old meadowland undamaged by farming improvements. These include adder's-tongue, great burnet, common meadow rue, pepper saxifrage and creeping-Jenny.

The opposite bank along this stretch is much less accessible and for this reason provides a haven for many birds including mallard, moorhens and coots. Mute swans regularly nest in sites such as Iffley Island, and kingfishers and herons are seen.

Iffley Lock on the River Thames

The riverside track continues downstream and the Thames assumes an ever more rural character in spite of its proximity to the suburbs of Oxford until, eventually, Isis Tavern is reached.

Iffley Lock and the Isis Tavern are popular destinations for excursions from Oxford. The Isis Tavern is another riverside pub containing memorabilia of university boat races but also boasts the only old English nine-pin bowling alley in Oxford. A converted farmhouse with pleasant gardens, it makes an ideal first stop, offering real ale, lunchtime bar meals and a chance to contemplate a stretch of the river rowed upon by Lewis Carroll (Charles Dodgson) and the real "Alice In Wonderland", the young daughter of the Dean of Christchurch.

A short distance from the Isis Tavern the path crosses over an attractive and substantial stone bridge to Iffley Lock which, together with Sandford-on-Thames, the next lock downriver, were the first two pound-locks built on the Thames, although both have since been rebuilt.

Notice, on the right between the lock and the river-bank, a system for hauling small boats over rollers that avoids the time consuming process of using the lock. Apart from a chance to rest or picnic whilst being entertained by "boating business", Iffley lock also provides access, via a

Iffley Rectory, door to street

path over the lock and weir, to one of the finest and most complete examples of a Norman church in all England.

Those wishing to visit this church should follow the lane from the other side of the river and turn right at the T junction and up a slight hill at the top of which, on the right, stands St Mary the Virgin church, built in the reign of Henry II (1154-1189). This small, twelfth-century parish church, together with the adjoining twelfth/thirteenth-century rectory, presents a unity, a feeling of "rightness" which has to be seen to be truly experienced. For those for whom a brief visit is not enough, part of the rectory is now available for holiday lets through The Landmark Trust.

When returning to the lock, a small stone will be noticed where the path turns right over the weir which records the fate of the mill which once stood on this site.

From the lock the route turns right over a wooden bridge and then left along the river bank before reaching the road bridge which marks the end of the Iffley Meadows Nature Reserve. The bridge also marks the end of the well surfaced track followed this far downstream which now becomes more like a field path, muddy in places even in fine weather. A wooden footbridge precedes an iron

The Kings Arms, Sandford-on-Thames Lock

girder railway bridge on the other side of which a wooden swing gate leads to the path which now runs across open pastures. Here the path is set back from the river-bank and, shortly after a house built on an island on the opposite side of the river is passed, it cuts across a bend in the river which it rejoins where it turns left over a gated iron footbridge. A further bridge of the same type brings the path back to the bankside proper. From here it runs over a small bridge next to a weir before reaching an open pasture on the other side of which is the lock at Sandford-on-Thames.

Sandford Lock is the deepest on the river above Teddington and is sited next to the large buildings of what used to be a paper mill.

Here the route crosses to the other side of the the river on a path which runs across the top of the lock and over a wooden footbridge to turn left along the front of the King's Arm's. At the end of the attractive riverside gardens behind the pub, a wooden gate on the right marks where the Oxbridge route finally parts company with the Thames.

From here the route first crosses the car park and then turns left up the road. At the top of the slight hill, on the left, stands a small church whose porch was restored by Dame Eliza Isham in 1652.

Above the porch is the following inscription: Thanks to thy charitie religious dame, which found mee olde and made mee new again".

At the T junction with the main road the route turns right past a pub called The Catherine Wheel. It then turns at the first left, on a road signposted to Henley, which runs under another main road before reaching a roundabout in front of Oxford's new Science Park. From here the route takes a footpath just above a bus stop to the right of the roundabout signposted "Garsington, three miles". The path runs past the front entrances of a mobile home site, then turns right just in front of the main entrance of a sewage treatment works. From here the path follows the metal perimeter fence, turning left behind the works and staying with the wire fence on the right after the works has been passed.

Apart from field and game birds, gulls and the occasional heron are attracted here, especially in the winter months.

The path now becomes a track which runs for a good mile across wide, arable fields with the Cowley car factories in the distance on the left and a line of pylons running parallel on the right. The track carries on ahead where it is joined by another coming in from the left and after a short distance, right at a T junction. It then turns left, just short of the line of pylons, and continues ahead, ignoring other tracks coming in from the left and right, and crosses straight over a small lane.

From here the route follows a headland bridleway down to the corner of the field where a metal swing gate leads to a field path across a pasture to a stile next to a road. It turns right along the road for a few yards and then left through a gateway along a bridleway known as Kiln Lane. At the end of this short lane the route turns right along a road leading uphill to the village of Garsington. Almost at the top of the hill, where the roadside path rises steeply above the level of the road, the route doubles back on itself for a few yards and then turns right on a way-marked footpath up the side of a house.

Those wishing to visit the village before continuing should follow the road ahead.

Garsington's church has fine views since it is built on the highest ridge between Oxford and the Chilterns. Amongst other memorials in the church is one by Eric Gill to Lady Ottoline Morrell who, from 1915 to 1927, lived at the southern end of the village in a Jacobean manor house, Garsington Manor. In her time she was a celebrated hostess whose soirees were attended by writers, artists and intellectuals such as T.S.Eliot, Virginia Woolf, D.H.Lawrence and Bertrand Russell. (Aldous Huxley was a frequent guest and the Manor House is said to be the setting for his book Chrome Yellow.) Today, the house is better known for the open air opera performed on its terrace, with picnics on the lawns or by the Italian Pool. Walkers in search of plainer fare need look no further than one of the three village pubs.

The route follows the footpath up the side of the house and, after a stile, the path bears left up the rise and across an arable field to a stile set in the hedge on the crest of the hill.

From here there are panoramic views across the city of Oxford beyond which the Cotswolds fringe a broad sweep of landscape. To the south-east the Chilterns can plainly be seen - a good place from which to bid the city a final farewell before facing north-east and the distant prospect of Cambridge.

From here the path runs downhill across a small pasture to another stile set back from a lane. Over the stile the route turns right for about 50 yards and then left where a finger-post indicates a path to the hamlet of Denton. From here a short track runs down through a gateway next to a garage before another stile after which the path crosses a small pasture.

Across the valley can be seen the neo-Gothic buildings of the theological college at Cuddesdon.

From here the path keeps to the left of the hedge before switching to the other side via a stile. It then continues to follow the hedge down to a stile in the bottom corner of the field after which it runs diagonally right across an arable field to a double stile and footbridge over a deep, sunken ditch. From here it crosses a pasture aiming for the electricity pole in the middle of the field, then crosses another stile down to a stile set in the corner of the field next to a large oak tree.

On the other side of the narrow pasture ahead can be seen the original east window of Brasenose College Chapel, brought here during alterations to the college in 1844/45, and built into the wall which surrounds the grounds of Denton House.

From here the path follows the fence and crosses one more stile before leading down to a small lane. The route turns right along the lane and then almost immediately left on a path running alongside a high stone wall. After about a hundred yards, it turns left over a stream to arrive at the small green in the hamlet of Denton. On the other side of the green faced by attractive cottages, the route turns left along the lane and up a hill, at the top of which it follows the High Street through the village of Cuddesdon.

Cuddesdon is well-known for its Anglican Theological College founded in 1856 and now known as Ripon College. On the opposite side of the road to the college buildings stand modern houses built on the site of the large house, burnt down in 1960, which served as the official residence of the Bishops of Oxford for 400 years. The substantial parish church of All Saints, partly rebuilt in the 1840s, owes much of its past importance to the proximity of the Bishops' official residence and contains many fine monuments to them. Being set on a high plateau, there are splendid views from the church and the village over the surrounding countryside with the distant Chilterns to the south-east.

The Bat and Ball Inn provides the first chance of B+B accommodation since leaving Oxford.

On leaving Cuddesdon, the route follows the small lane to the right of the church which leads down into the valley where Cuddeson Mill stands on the bank of the River Thame.

Cuddesdon Mill was rebuilt about 1800 on the site of a much earlier mill, (1066), which belonged to Abingdon Abbey. The original mill included a fish inclosure and was the cause of much strife with the Bishop of Lincoln's tenants in nearby Great Milton. They attempted to destroy the mill inclosure on several occasions, including one attempt when it is recorded that their plans were foiled "by Abbot Ealdred with the aid of the miraculous bones of St Vincent".

The crossing of the river also marks the route's first encounter with the River Thame which flows south from here to eventually join the Thames at Dorchester.

After crossing the mill-stream and river, the route stays with the lane up the other side of the valley. At the T junction it first turns right and then leaves the road on the left, opposite a barn, along the line of a headland path. Keeping to the left of the hedge the path runs down to a stile in the corner after which it follows the fence on the right for a few yards to stone steps set each side of the fence. From here the path runs diagonally right across a pasture, down a dip to a double stile and footbridge over a small stream. On the other side of the stream it runs uphill to a gate next to which a large stone set on its side has to be negotiated in order to reach the road where the route turns right into the village of Great Milton.

Great Milton has an unspoilt village green in its centre around which are clustered attractive thatched cottages and two of its three inns, The Bull and The Bell.

From here the nearest B+B accommodation is at Little Milton, about a mile further along the route.

GENERAL INFORMATION

En Route

Of Particular Interest	River Thames
	Iffley - Norman Church
	Iffley and Sandford-on-Thames - locks
	Garsington - viewpoint over the city
	Cuddesdon - Theological College; Water-mill
Accommodation	Cuddesdon only - The Bat and Ball Inn (01865) 874379
Refreshments	Iffley Lock - the Isis pub
	Sandford-on-Thames - three pubs
	Garsington - three pubs
	Cuddesdon - the Bat and Ball Inn
PO/shop	Garsington only
Public phone	Sandford-on-Thames, Garsington, Cuddesdon
Banks	None
Parking	Sandford-on-Thames, off-road
	Garsington, roadside only
	Cuddesdon, roadside only

Great Milton

Of particular interest	St Mary's church
	Great House, restaurant
Accommodation (nearest)	Little Milton (1 mile SW of Great Milton A329)
	Wits End, Little Milton (01844) 279281
	Manor House, Little Milton (01844) 279368

AN OXBRIDGE WALK

Camping	Piers Farm, Great Milton (01844) 279352 (Half a mile to the right from the T junction after Cuddesdon Mill - must phone in advance)
Refreshments	Three pubs
PO/village shop	Yes
Public phone	Yes
Bank	No
Parking	Roadside or round green only
Access	Road East of Oxford A40(T)
	Rail As Oxford
	Bus As Oxford

GREAT MILTON - GREAT HASELEY - TETSWORTH - MORETON - THAME - (9 miles)

Of particular interest

Great Haseley church, Manor House; thatched cottages; Thame church; many historic buildings, inc.working forge.

From the village green the route follows the road, bearing right between The Bull and The Bell, keeping left where the road forks and then past St Peter's church.

The church contains a tomb with the alabaster figures of Sir Michael Dormer, Lord Mayor of London, who died in 1616, together with his wife and father, all under a gilded canopy. Above the tomb hangs Sir Michael's helmet and sword. Next to the church stands a fourteenth-century manor house, now much altered to accommodate a well-known and exclusive restaurant, Le Manoir Aux Quat' Saisons. On the other side of the road can be seen the early Georgian facade of the seventeenth-century Great House. However, of this impressive trio of buildings it must be said that the church is kept locked, the restaurant is prohibitively expensive and the Great House can only be admired from a distance.

At the T junction the route crosses straight over the main road to follow the track opposite heading south over wide, arable fields. Across the fields to the north can be seen an unrestored windmill with one surviving sail. When the cross-tracks is reached the route turns left heading for a cluster of barns.

Turn right here for B+B at Wits End or Manor House in the

OXFORD TO THAME

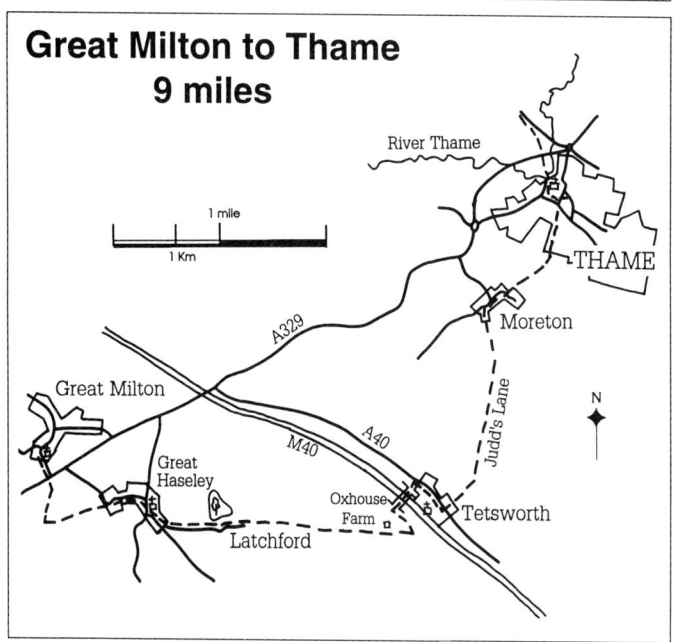

village of Little Milton, visible across the fields a short distance away.

Past the barns the track leads to a road where the route continues ahead through the village of Great Haseley.

Great Haseley is one of Oxfordshire's best kept-secrets. By-passed by history, tourism and the motorway, its pub, thatched cottages and stone houses sleep on undisturbed. Around the large church, with its thirteenth-century chancel and Norman door, is grouped an impressive manor house, and a church farm complete with medieval tithe barn.

At the T junction in the centre of the village the route turns right. Then, after a hundred yards or so, left along a drive marked "Private road - Footpath only" which leads to the church. From the church it turns right on a track and then left along a lane. At the fork the route keeps to the left along Latchford Lane, a narrow farm road

AN OXBRIDGE WALK

which runs between often high hedges for about a mile to Latchford House and Farm. Past the farm, just before another farmhouse, the road becomes a track where it turns left through a white gate. The track then bears right and left past a large double barn and graveyard for old agricultural machinery. From here the track continues ahead keeping to the right of the hedge until a gap is reached where it switches to the other side of the hedge. It then follows the hedge-line to the next corner where it turns right along the edge of the field keeping to the left of the hedge past a gap. At the next corner, the track continues ahead between high hedges (ignoring gaps to the right and left). Where the hedges end, the track emerges into a large pasture and, keeping to the right of the hedge, the route climbs to the top of the hill in front.

As higher ground is reached, good views open up to the south-east and the distant Chilterns.

After passing Oxhouse Farm and bungalow on the left, the route continues ahead downhill through two metal field-gates. At the second gate it turns left to follow a path keeping to the right of the hedge before crossing two stiles and two footbridges in the corner of the field. It then follows the hedge on the right along the edge of the field until a gate is reached where it turns sharply left across the pasture to a stile in the opposite hedge. From here the route turns right along a track leading across an access bridge over the M40. On the other side of the bridge the track keeps straight ahead until meeting the road where the route turns right.

The two houses immediately to the left where the track meets the road both provide B+B and one also has camping facilities.

Having turned right from the track the route follows the road through the centre of the village of Tetsworth.

Tetsworth was once important as the first staging-post on the Oxford to London coach route. This stretch was also particularly dangerous for well-heeled travellers setting out on what was then a hazardous journey and many were relieved of their valuables by highwaymen lying in wait on dark and lonely stretches of the road. Three coaches a day to and from the capital stopped at The Swan, whose seventeenth- and eighteenth-century facade conceals an even older interior. Road traffic dwindled in the 1840s with the coming of the railways and this once famous hostellry went into decline.

Ironically, what finally finished it off was not the railways, but the postwar development of the motorways network and the by-passing of the village by the M40. A prominent, boarded-up building, it still stands as a relic of the days when heavy traffic at least meant plenty of passing trade.

Tetsworth is a much quieter village now, with its village green overlooked by its surviving pub, The Lion on the Green (B+B available). The Oxfordshire Way comes into the village at its southern end, via a pedestrian underpass under the M40, and leaves in a northerly direction from the other side of the village green.

The route follows the road through the centre of the village, past the village green and the boarded-up Swan. About a hundred yards up the hill from the Swan, the route leaves the road on the left via Judd's Lane, up the right-hand side of the village primary school.

Judd's Lane is a track with a good surface which runs for about 2 miles across rolling pastures with fine views of the surrounding countryside where it crosses Horsenden Hill. Later it becomes metalled where it serves as an access road for the two or three farms passed.

Eventually, the hamlet of Moreton is reached, which offers both B+B accommodation and a campsite.

The route continues ahead following the lane past the old ex-pub on the right and the memorial cross on the left. When a small pond on the right is reached, it turns left down a short cul-de-sac at the end of which a path leads off to the right of Brook Cottage. From here a metalled path runs over several fields before joining a track known as Bates Leys, which leads ahead to the outskirts of Thame. On reaching the road the route turns left past the recreation field and up to a roundabout. It then runs ahead to the right, down another cul-de-sac at the end of which a short path leads to Thame High Street, immediately opposite the Town Hall and the Tourist Information Office.

Thame first became a market town in the thirteenth century. In the past the market was crucial to the town's prosperity and at one time was the third most important market in the county. Today, evidence of past prosperity can be seen in the buildings which line its broad high street, the widest in Oxfordshire. All periods of architecture are represented from the fifteenth century to date, including solid Georgian houses and famous inns such as The Spread Eagle. A working forge in the High Street making iron door-

*Punch door-stop,
Thame Forge*

stops etc. is open to visitors. *The Victorian Town Hall, which projects into the High Street and houses the Tourist Information Centre on its ground floor, has a leaflet entitled "A Walk Around Thame" containing detailed information about the town's history, buildings and past residents of note.*

St Mary's church stands in the oldest part of the town and was itself begun in the thirteenth century. Amongst much else of interest, the church contains some fine table tombs, including one belonging to Richard Quartermain who built nearby Rycote Chapel. However, for theatrical effect, nothing approaches the magnificence of the tomb of Lord Williams and his wife, situated as it is, right in the centre of the chancel in front of the altar. Another tomb, on the right-hand wall of the chancel, belongs to Sir John Clerke, knighted by Henry VIII. It is his helmet which hangs high up on the wall and, below a small alcove in the wall, a brass plaque set in the floor records further details of his family. (According to some recent visitors to the church, Sir John's descendants emigrated to America in 1638 and their descendants are currently alive and well and living in Kentucky.) Outside, to the west of the church can be seen the imposing prewar gatehouse to the Prebendal House, whose chapel dates from 1234. The Prebendal passed into private hands at the dissolution of Thame Abbey in 1539. A fuller description of the church can be found in an information sheet and recently completed guide on sale in the church shop. The church is open for visitors Mon to Sat, 11am and 4pm.

Column of Victory, Blenheim Park, Woodstock

Memorial Gardens, Christ Church
Blenheim Park, Woodstock

OXFORD TO THAME

GENERAL INFORMATION

En Route

Of particular interest	Great Haseley church, Manor House, thatched cottages
Accommodation	Tetsworth - The Croft, 2 High St (01844) 281494
	Little Acre, 4 High St (01844) 281423
	Lion on the Green pub (01844) 281274
	Moreton - Vine Cottage (01844) 216910
Camping	Tetsworth - The Croft, 2 High St (01844) 281494
	Moreton - The Dairy (farm) (01844) 214075
Refreshments	Great Haseley - one pub
	Tetsworth - one pub
PO/shops	Tetsworth - PO/stores, antiques, tapestry/art
Public phone	Great Haseley, Tetsworth
Banks	None (nearest, Thame)
Parking	Great Haseley - roadside only
	Tetsworth - off-road but no car park

Thame

Of particular interest	St Mary's church
	Many historic buildings including working forge
Accommodation	The Haven, 5 Oxford Rd (01844) 212809
	The Blackhorse Hotel (01844) 212886
	The Four Horseshoes, Park St (01844) 212029
	Wellington Hotel, Wellington St (01844) 216010
Refreshments	Restaurants, pubs
PO/shops	Yes (including outdoor and camping)
Public phones	Yes
Banks	Yes
Parking	Short and long stay car parks
Market days	Street - Tues, Cattle - Wed, Fri
Tourist information	Town Hall (01844) 212834
	Open Mon - Fri, 8.30am-5.00pm
Access	Road A418 (Oxford to Aylesbury)
	M40 (junction 7)
	Rail Nearest station, Haddenham and Thame Parkway (01494) 441561
	Bus (01296) 84919, (01865) 711312

AN OXBRIDGE WALK

BUCKINGHAMSHIRE
THAME - LEIGHTON BUZZARD

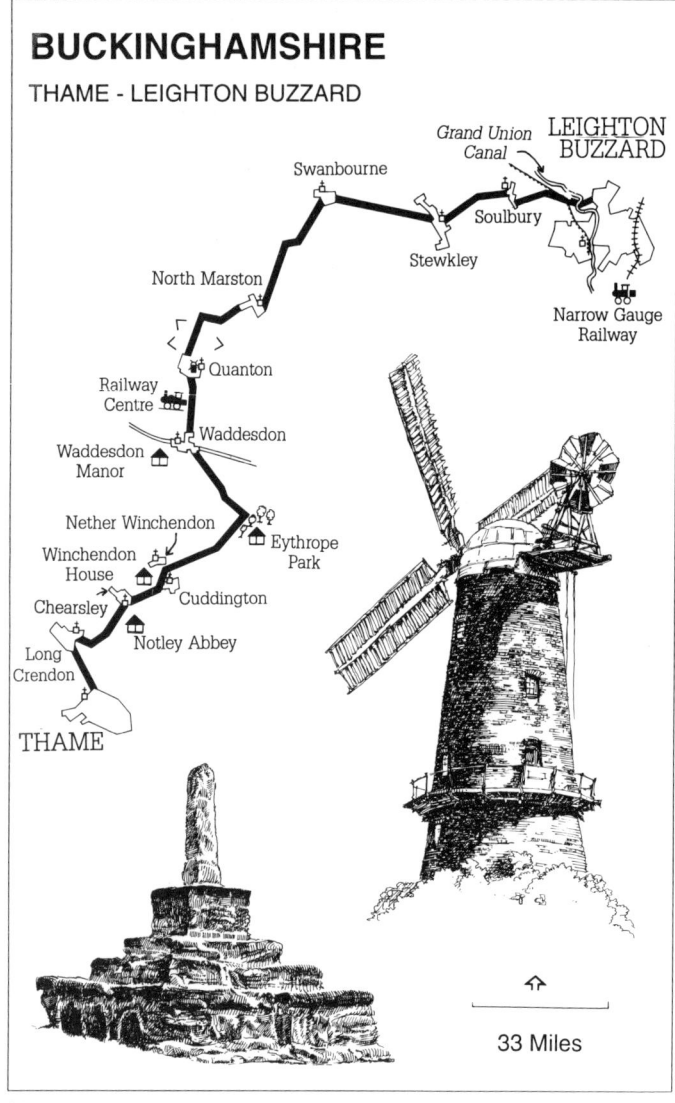

33 Miles

Thame to Leighton Buzzard: 33 miles

THAME - LONG CRENDON - CHEARSLEY - CUDDINGTON -
(7 miles)

Of particular interest

Long Crendon - Old Court House (National Trust); Notley Abbey and dovecote; Chearsley church; Cuddington church and plaque on churchyard wall.

From the Tourist Information Centre the route follows the High Street towards the church. Opposite the Six Bells pub, it turns right down Church Road at the bottom of which it passes the old tithe barn on the left before running through the churchyard and down steps to the road opposite the prebendary. Here it turns right past the church following the old road, now closed, via a bridge over the River Thame.
 Here the river marks the boundary between Oxfordshire and Buckinghamshire and there is a marker on the right-hand side half-way across the bridge.
 Within a short distance the old road carries straight over the busy A418 and about a hundred yards further along the road, the Thame Valley Walk from Tiddington comes in on the left. Further on, the old road joins the B4011, where the route turns left on the roadside path. It then stays with the road for about a mile eventually running up a hill at the top of which it turns right along the High Street of Long Crendon.

Long Crendon more than repays the effort of the roadside walk. Selected as the quintessential English village for the postwar Festival of Britain in London, 1951, it has no fewer than 114 buildings listed as being of Special Architectural or Historic Interest, including 18 "Cruck" buildings and about 50 thatched houses. In the spring the whole village is involved in the annual production of the York cycle of Mystery Plays and for this week villagers may be seen in public places in medieval dress. A modestly priced

**Thame to Cuddington
7 miles**

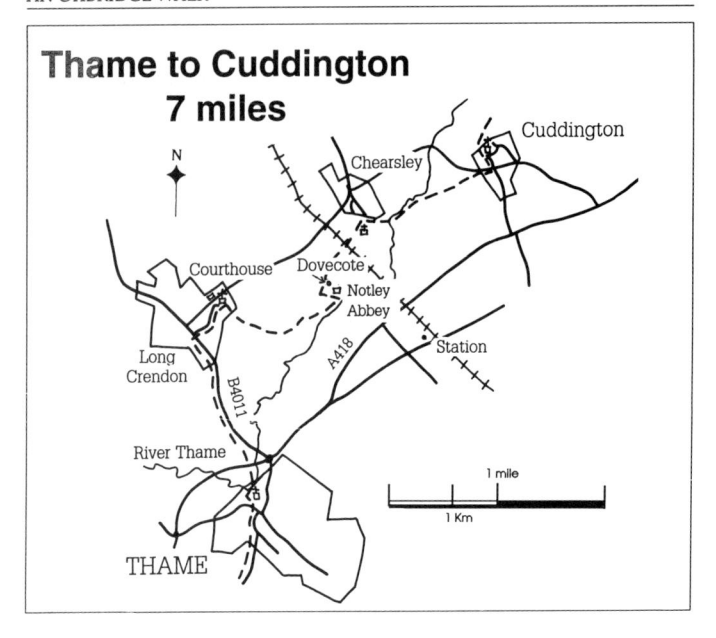

leaflet to a guided walk around the village, available from the village post office, lists 54 points of interest.

B+B is available at the Star Inn and at No 2, Highfield.

The High Street is lined with cottages some of which still have the built-in special cupboards which were used in connection with the needlemaking industry which thrived here in the eighteenth century. At the end of the High Street is the church of St Mary's, parts of which date back to the thirteenth century. In medieval times the village was an important wool trade centre and to the left of the church stands the Court House which was originally connected with the cloth trade and in which manorial courts were held. In 1900, the Court House, complete with poltergeist, was the first building to be acquired by the National Trust. The upper floor is open to the public, Apr-Sept, Wed 2-6pm, Sun and Bank Hol 11am-6pm

Teas are available from nearby Church House on most Sat and Sun.

From in front of the Court House and church the Oxbridge route descends into and along the Thame Valley following the way-marked Thame Valley Walk as far as Eythrope Park.

Thame Valley Walk, Long Crendon

The Thame Valley Walk is way-marked to the right, down Church Green Lane at the end of the High Street, just in front of the church. The path runs past the seventeenth-century Manor House on the left down Cop Hill through a small wooden gate to follow a field path ahead over a rough pasture to a metal gate in the corner of the field. From here the path turns left along a headland path keeping to the right of the hedge for the next three fields until a footbridge and stile is reached. The path then bears right over a large arable field heading for a stile next to another metal gate almost in the top right-hand corner.

This is the closest that the path comes to the River Thame for some distance and, having crossed the stile, it is worth walking over to inspect the small weir and sluices above the bridge; all that remains of a substantial brick watermill which stood here until well into this century.

Over the stile the route turns left along the fence for a few yards, then left back over the fence on the other side of which it turns right following the fence and the trees bordering the river. The path then goes over two more stiles each side of a narrow belt of trees to run ahead over a small pasture aiming for a stile set in the hedgerow to the front of what remains of Notley Abbey.

Notley Abbey was founded in 1162 by Augustinian monks and was one of the richest monasteries in the country until the dissolution in 1538. Nothing now remains of the great church, at least twice the length of the present Oxford Cathedral, which formed part of the complex of buildings that stood here.

However, some idea of the scale and grandeur of the original abbey can be gained from the buildings which have survived, since the building which stands today was once merely the Abbot's lodging and guest house! The octagonal tower which can be seen from the footpath is a sixteenth-century staircase tower.

From 1947 to 1962 Notley Abbey was the home of Sir Laurence Olivier and his wife, Vivien Leigh. In his autobiography Sir Laurence admits to loving this place more than his friends or even his career and famous guests to the Abbey, such as David Niven, later recalled how much Sir Laurence enjoyed playing the role of village squire. Strange, in this quiet corner of rural England, to imagine "Scarlet O'Hara" picnicking on the lawns - not so strange, perhaps, to imagine Sir Laurence declaiming lines from Henry V at the battle of Agincourt on the riverbank!

Today, the Abbey and its grounds remain in private ownership; it is not open to the public and there is no public access to the river at this point.

From the stile, the route turns left on a fenced in path next to the drive to Notley Abbey, at the end of which a stile gives access to the

Dovecote, Notley Abbey

farm-road leading uphill to Notley Farm. After passing the farmhouse a cross-track is reached where the Thame Valley Walk crosses to turn right behind the barns and silos to arrive opposite a large, square stone dovecote, which is well worth a closer look.

Probably built to supply food for the monks in the nearby monastery, the dovecote's main structure was repaired and reinforced in 1970, European Conservation Year. The outside of the building gives few clues to its original function, but an opening on the far side allows entrance. Once inside, the purpose of the building is obvious with the remains of thousands of stone roosts lining the ancient walls of what was, in effect, a medieval high-rise for doves. Today, only a few pigeons lurk in the roof timbers but, though few in number, they have a way of letting the unwary intruder know about what must have been a considerable problem in the days when 4000 pairs of birds occupied the building!

Outside there are fine views over the surrounding countryside with the Chilterns to the south on the distant skyline.

From the electricity pole in front of the dovecote, the route runs downhill keeping to the left of the hedge. At the bottom of the slope, the path continues in the same direction across a small pasture to a stile, from where it heads right across another pasture to cross a footbridge into Long Mead Copse.

This small wood of pollarded willows, poplars, oak, ash and alder provides a breeding site for woodpeckers and a shady refuge for plants such as ragged robin.

The path follows the stream through the copse on the other side of which it goes straight over a farm track and a stile. From here the path follows the fence line up to and across a railway line opened in 1910 as part of the Great Western Railway's new line to Birmingham. The path continues ahead keeping to the right of the fence-line and shortly expands to a track across the "pick your own" fields of a soft-fruit farm. The fruit fields end at a metal gate where the route continues ahead over a farm-track and stile then across a small pasture and down a bank to Church Lane on the outskirts of Chearsley. From here the route turns right down the lane past the church (turn left for the pub or B+B accommodation at Manor Farm).

Chearsley, like Long Crendon, occupies a hilltop position, built on isolated hills formed where the more resistant Portland limestone overlies the softer clays of the Aylesbury Vale. The village has a small green, a pub and a post office/village stores.

The church of St Nicholas is of light grey local limestone with a tiled roof. Plain, homely and well cared for, it is described by the information sheet inside the church as "the simple church of a farming village, used by countless generations of tenant farmers, yeoman and labourers, their hard-working wives and many children".

The route continues past the church and where the lane ends the Oxbridge route parts company with the Thame Valley Walk for the next 2 miles or so in order to include a very pleasant walk by the river into Cuddington. Where the lane ends, therefore, the route carries straight on and, after a few yards, turns right via a wooden swing-gate next to a finger-post to Cuddington. From here the path bears left over a pasture to cross a footbridge over the Thame, on the other side of which it turns left to follow the willow tree-lined river-bank. At the end of a long, narrow pasture, the path crosses to a stile in the top, right-hand corner, then heads diagonally right over a second field aiming for a gap in the hedge. It then continues in the same direction down the centre of another long pasture aiming for a stile in the top right-hand corner next to a gate. From here the route follows a track which runs up the rise in front to where it eventually meets and turns right along the road into Cuddington. The route stays with the road as far as the village green where it turns left down Upper Church Street just before The Crown pub (B+B available).

Cuddington is sited on a rolling ridge-top; a small, attractive village, with thatched cottages and a pub clustered round a village green complete with a village pump. This is "wychert" country, a type of wall building incorporating chalky marl and chopped straw, similar to West Country Cobb. Such walls are surprisingly durable providing they have a "good hat and a stout pair of shoes" - that is a dry, limestone base and a thatched or tiled top. The church of St Nicholas is partly built of local limestone with the later addition of a fourteenth-century porch and fifteenth-century tower, and was restored in 1857. Today, the church in its typically English village setting, forms a pretty enough picture, but any romantic notions about village life in the past are quickly dispelled by the plaque on the wall in the churchyard to the right of the main entrance. This records the death by "Asiatic Cholera" of 48 persons in August 1849, in the nearby hamlet of Gibralter.

GENERAL INFORMATION

En Route

Of particular interest	Long Crendon - Old Court House (National Trust)
	Notley Abbey and dovecote
	Chearsley - St Nicholas Church
Accommodation	Long Crendon - The Angel Inn (01844) 208268
	2, Highfield (01844) 208111
	Chearsley - Manor Farm (01844) 208303
Refreshments	Long Crendon - five pubs, Chinese restaurant
	Chearsley - one pub
PO/shops	Long Crendon - PO, stores, delicatessen
	Chearsley - PO/store
Public phone	Long Crendon, Chearsley
Banks	None
Parking	Long Crendon - in the village square
	Chearsley - roadside or church car park

Cuddington

Of particular interest	St Nicholas's church - plaque on wall in churchyard
Accommodation	The Crown pub (01844) 292222
Refreshments	One pub plus Annie Bailey's Ale and Eating House
PO/shop	Yes
Public phone	Yes
Bank	No (nearest, Waddesdon)
Parking	Roadside only
Access	Road N off A418 between Aylesbury and Thame
	Rail Nearest station - Haddenham & Thame Parkway Chiltern Line, London to Banbury (01494) 441561
	Bus (01296) 84919

CUDDINGTON - LOWER WINCHENDON - EYTHROPE PARK - WADDESDON - QUAINTON - (9 miles)

Of particular interest

Lower Winchendon - Winchendon House; Eythrope Park; Waddesdon - Waddesdon Manor; Quainton - Buckinghamshire Railway Centre, Quainton Tower Windmill.

From the church the route crosses over the road and down Tibbys Lane to follow the circular walk path to Nether Winchendon. At the bottom of the lane, the path runs down past a thatched cottage before turning left over a concrete footbridge and then right along a headland path. After bearing right, the path runs straight ahead over three arable fields and stiles before crossing a wooden footbridge over the River Thame. From here the path leads to the rear of an old watermill standing on the site of a mill mentioned in the Domesday Book. The path runs across the front of the mill, now converted into a house, and rejoins the route of the Thame Valley Walk where it turns right skirting the end of the farm buildings.

Before continuing, it is worth turning left and following the drive away from the mill for a short distance, in order to pay a brief visit to the hamlet of Lower Winchendon.

Nether or Lower Winchedon once belonged to Notley Abbey and is notable for its manor house, church and attractive, thatched cottages. In the eighteenth-century Winchendon House was the home of Sir Francis Bernard, the last British Governor of New Jersey and Massachusetts. The church of Saint Nicholas dates mainly from the fifteenth century and has largely escaped subsequent "improvements". It has box pews and a high pulpit, as well as candelabra, English and Flemish glass, and brasses, including one of a twentieth-century officer. The early eighteenth-century clock in the tower has a 14ft pendulum and its blue exterior face only has a single hand.

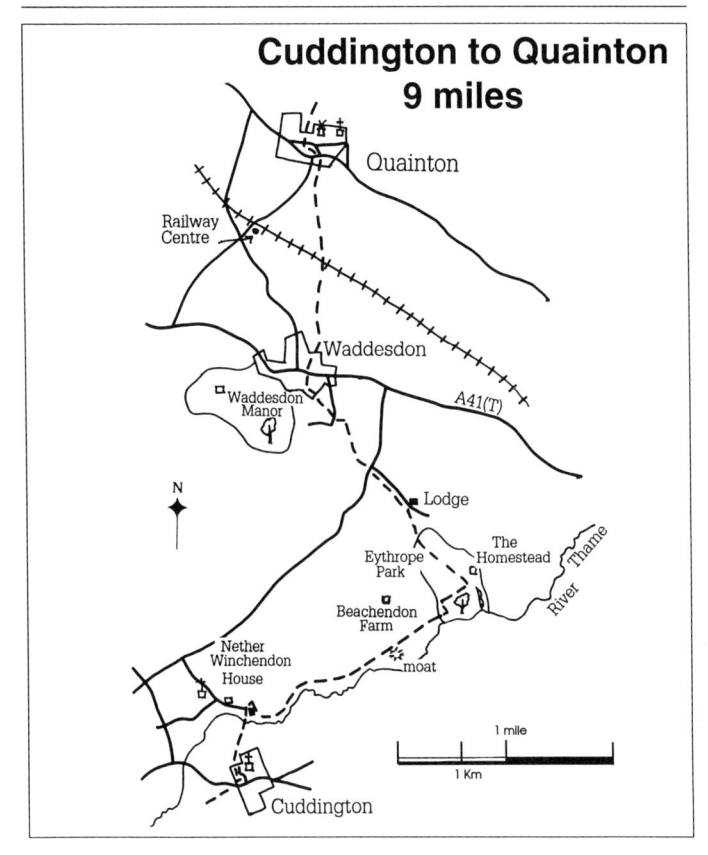

Having turned right to skirt the farm buildings, the route goes over a stile on the left-hand side of a large barn. From here it follows the way-mark signs for the Thame Valley Walk and bears left and then ahead down a long pasture keeping to the right of the hedge and running roughly parallel with the river on the right. At the end of this field the path turns left over a stile and along a fenced-in track which turns right and, after a few hundred yards, emerges on open pastures again. From here the path carries on ahead over a succession of stiles and pastures before arriving at a footbridge and stile in front of a huge arable field stretching up the hill to the left and almost down to the river on the right. The path crosses the field aiming to the right of the lone oak tree in the lower half of the field and, having reached the other side, goes through the hedge and across a wide pasture keeping to the left of the remains of an old moat overlooked by Beachendon Farm on top of the hill to the north. The path keeps more or less straight ahead across several arable fields, aiming for the left-hand side of a small wood. Eventually, it joins the farm-road to Beachendon Farm and crosses over a cattle grid and through farm-gate to arrive at the Bridge Lodge entrance to Eythrope Park. Here an oak finger-post marks the conjunction of the Thame Valley Walk, the North Bucks Way, the Swan's Way, and, the latest addition to the network of long-distance footpaths, the Midshires Way.

The Oxbridge route turns left, through a second gateway to follow the North Bucks/Swan's/Midshires Way along the metalled drive into the Park.

Eythrope Park surrounds The Pavilion, one of the five great houses built in the Vale of Aylesbury by the Rothschilds in the second half of the nineteenth century. Built in 1883 for Alice de Rothschild. it was originally built without bedrooms for use as a very grand summer-house, but after Alice died in 1922, bedrooms were added and the house has remained a family home ever since.

Before continuing along the route, it is worth following the drive in front for about a hundred yards to see the small stone bridge built over this arm of the Thame standing in front of a lake created when the watercourse was dammed in the 1880s.

Having turned left through the gateway and along the drive in front of Bridge Lodge, the Oxbridge route follows the Swan's/

Midshires Way along the drive where it bends right in front of a small house, and after a few hundred yards crosses straight over a crossroads.

The right-hand turning at the crossroads leads to the Pavilion, but the house cannot be seen as it is surrounded by high hedges and trees.

After the crossroads, the route continues for a few hundred yards more before turning left at some giant redwoods with the "Homestead" plainly in sight at the end of the drive. From here the path soon becomes a good, wide track leading across arable fields.

Eventually, a plantation of new trees is reached on the right at the end of which the route turns right along the North Bucks Way.

From here the route follows the way-marks for the North Bucks/Midshires Way as far as the top of Quainton Hill.

A short hill completes the climb out of the Thame Valley and there are good views across the countryside to the south. The track then continues ahead as far as North Lodge, which marks the limit of Eythrope Park. From here the route continues along a small lane over Waddesdon Hill for about a quarter of a mile before crossing over a main road and through the entrance gates to Waddesdon Stud.

The path now runs down the left-hand side of an immaculate stables complex facing onto a manicured lawn after which it continues ahead down the side of a barn to where a wooden swing-gate leads to a path through a small wood. Via a stile on the other side of the wood, the path runs diagonally left over a small paddock from where there is a good view to the north of the next de Rothschild mansion, Waddesdon Manor. From a second stile on the other side of the paddock, the path runs downhill through a plantation of young trees and over a large stile almost at the bottom of the hill. It then continues as a headland track, with the comparative novelty of a newly planted hedge on the left, before crossing two further stiles each side of a small lane. After the lane, the path clips the corner of a field before going through trees and bears left past a back-garden and tennis court on the right. At the end of a large barn on the left the route turns right along a lane for a few yards and then left into a small wood. From here the path first crosses a bridge over a stream and then bears right to emerge at an arable field where it continues ahead aiming for the perimeter fence round school playing-fields. At the fence it turns right along the school perimeter and, about a hundred yards after the path becomes metalled, the route turns right over a way-marked stile. From here the path crosses allotments on the other side of which it turns right for a few yards and then left over a footbridge. A fenced path now leads into Baker Street where the route turns right down to and straight over the main A41. For the village of Waddesdon and Waddesdon Manor turn left along the main road.

Waddesdon endured years of rural decline prior to the arrival of the de Rothschilds and was far from being a prosperous village. Known as "Black Waddesdon", due to its hostile reception of travellers, it could be fairly said that the arrival of this famous and fabulously wealthy family was the best thing that ever happened to it. Largely demolished and rebuilt by Baron Ferdinand de Rothschild, little of the original village has survived apart from the church and the seventeenth-century Bell Inn. Many of the buildings from this era of rebuilding still bear the Rothschild family crest of a crown and five arrows surrounded by the latin motto Concordia, Industria, Integritas (Concord, Integrity and Industry). Originally from Frankfurt, the five arrows depicted in the crest commemorate the five sons of Mayer Amschel Rothschild (1744-1812) who spread the influence and wealth of this famous family throughout Europe. Today, the village is bisected by the busy A41 trunk road and generally unremarkable except for its church and nearby Waddesdon Manor, which was bequeathed by James de Rothschild to the National Trust in 1957.

Waddesdon Manor was built in the 1870s for Baron Ferdinand de Rothschild by Destailleur. The creation of a French style chateau in a Buckinghamshire setting was a major undertaking preceded by the flattening of the hill-top and the building of a tramway to nearby Quainton Road station. A team of Percheron mares imported specially from Normandy dragged wagon loads of yellow Bath stone for the house and fully grown trees to plant round it. Surrounded by acres of the finest late Victorian formal gardens and parks designed by Laine, the house has important collections of art, French royal furniture, Savonnerie carpets and Sevres porcelain. The parkland and grounds, which also contain an elegant cast iron Rococo style aviary and grotto, and the house, gift shop and tea rooms, are open to the public as follows:

THAME TO LEIGHTON BUZZARD

Waddesdon Manor

House: 31st Mar-16th Oct, Thurs-Sun, 1-6pm.
Grounds: Mar-Dec, Wed-Sun, 11am - 6pm.
Also open on public holidays. For further details (admission charges etc.) tel (01296) 651282.

Having crossed the main road, the route continues down a cul-de-sac and where this turns right a finger-post points the North Bucks Way ahead along a path sandwiched between a hedge and a high wooden fence. A stile takes the route clear of the houses and across more stiles each side of two fields of rough pasture to a footbridge, where the path leads diagonally left, aiming to the right of some farm buildings. After crossing a farm-road via two more stiles, the path follows the fence on the left and skirts a small pond before turning right along the fence. At an inconspicuous stile where the overhead electricity lines come in from the right the route turns left and then right on a concrete farm track. Where the track turns right the North Bucks Way continues ahead over a stile and down the length of a long pasture.

Ahead lies the village of Quainton and its conspicuous windmill, so from here the general line of the route is obvious.

At the top left-hand corner of the long pasture, the path crosses stiles each side of the old Metropolitan railway line and keeps to the right of the hedge across a narrow pasture before crossing a double stile and footbridge. The path continues ahead across a wide pasture aiming to the right of a gap in the hedge on the far side of the field. From here it carries on in the same direction over three more fields aiming to the right of the distant farm buildings. A last stile and footbridge takes the path past new houses squeezed in on the edge of the village then between hedges and houses on the outskirts of the village to arrive on the forecourt of the White Hart pub (B+B accommodation available).

Here the route turns left to follow the road for a few hundred yards and then heads diagonally right across the village green at the top left-hand corner of which it leaves the village via the road.

Quainton's village green has the remains of a fifteenth-century preaching cross and causeway and is dominated by the windmill just above it to the north. Near the church of The Holy Cross and St Mary, at the eastern end of the village, stands a row of picturesque seventeenth-century almshouses. The church itself is noted for the quality of its seventeenth- and eighteenth-century monuments, including a memorial plaque to George Lipscomb (1773-1846), Buckinghamshire's first historian. A booklet giving detailed information about the village and its history, including a guided walk, is on sale in the village shop in Church Street.

The Tower windmill is the tallest of its type in the county and is visible for miles. It was built by James Anstiss (1830-33) from locally made bricks, floor by floor, from the inside, without the use of scaffolding. It worked by wind-power until 1881 after which it was converted to steam-power and continued to operate until the beginning of this century. After falling into disrepair and near deriliction for many years, a group of local volunteers undertook the long process of its restoration in 1974. Due to their valiant efforts, and donations from both public and private sources, the sails have been restored and plans are in hand to re-install the gearing mechanism and grinding stones in the near future. The mill is currently open to visitors Sun 10am-1pm.

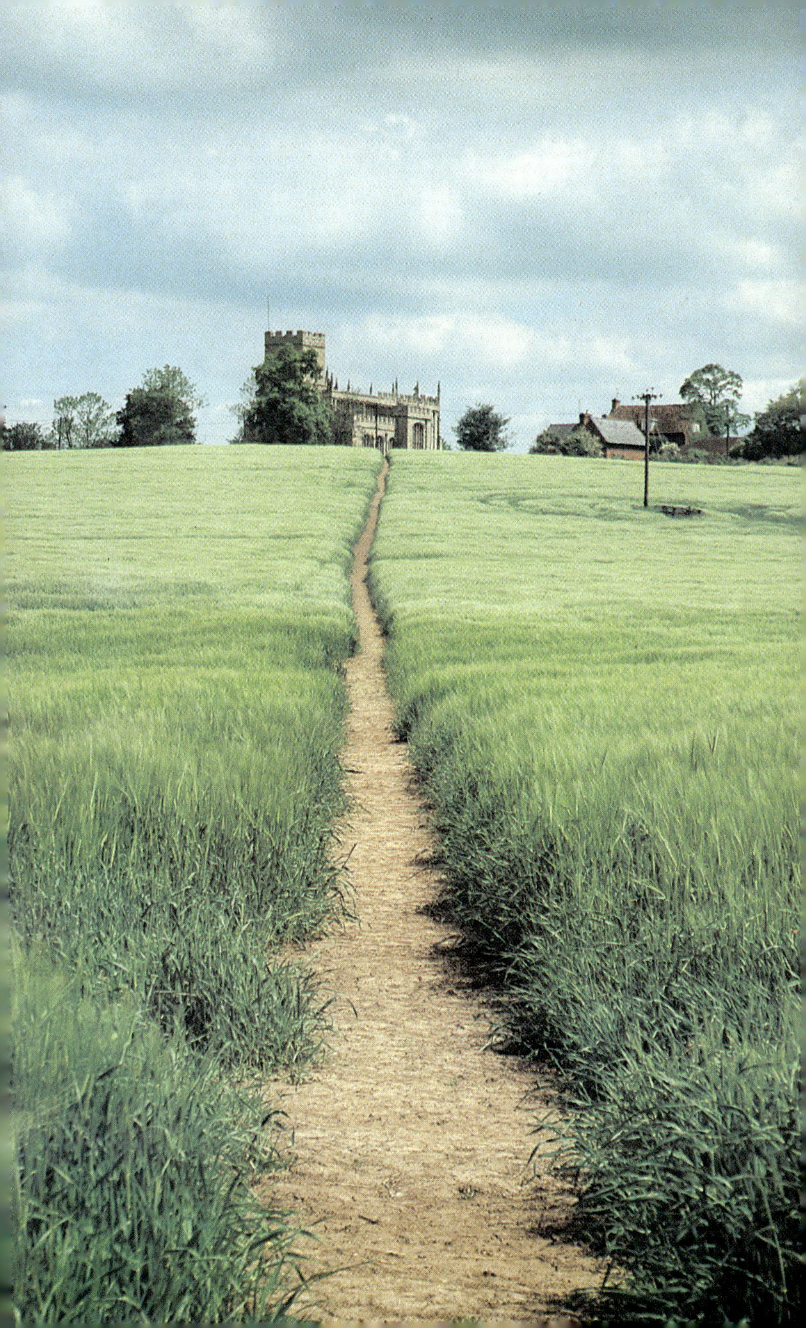

River Thame, Eythrope Park
Swan's Way/North Bucks Way, nr Eythrope (Alternative Route)

Windmill restoration volunteers, Quainton, 1993

Buckinghamshire Railway Centre is a 10min walk along the road to the south of the village at Quainton Road station, the last remaining station of the once mighty Metropolitan Railway. A tide of Victorian enthusiastic optimism carried its lines from the nation's capital deep into "Metroland", as far as nearby Verney Junction. All is now abandoned, much of the track dismantled and the country stations, except this one, turned into bijou residences for commuters to nearby towns. However, the roads may not have won the battle entirely as a major step towards the possibility of eventually restoring passenger services will be taken with the installation of points enabling access from the sidings to what is left of what was once the main line. Quainton may never become "the Crewe of Buckinghamshire" but as Betjeman also wrote in his poem of Dilton Marsh Halt:

> And when all the horrible roads are finally done for,
> And there's no more petrol left in the world to burn,
> Here to the Halt from Salisbury and from Bristol
> Steam trains will return.

The Centre's 25-acre site has on display one of the country's largest collections of historic steam and diesel locomotives, including coaching

AN OXBRIDGE WALK

Metropolitan 1

and freight rolling stock.

There is a small museum and, in addition to special events, the centre opens on the following basis:

Steaming days -   every Sun and Bank Hol Mon, Easter-end Oct.
*   Wed in Jun, Jul & Aug*

Non-steaming days - Sat, May-Oct
*   Sun, Nov, Jan-Mar.*

For further details tel (01296) 75450.

Metropolitan 1, Bucks Railway Centre

GENERAL INFORMATION

En Route

Of particular interest	Lower Winchendon - Winchendon House
	Eythrope Park
	Waddesdon - Waddesdon Manor
Accommodation	Five Arrows Hotel, Waddesdon (01296) 651727
	(No budget accommodation in Waddesdon)
Refreshments	Waddesdon only - three pubs, two restaurants
	(mobile cafe in lay-by just outside village)
PO/village shops	Waddesdon only
Public phone	Nether Winchendon, Waddesdon
Bank	Waddesdon only
Parking	Nether Winchendon - very limited
	Eythrope Park - none (private estate, private roads)
	Waddesdon - roadside
	Car park available for visitors to Waddesdon Manor

Quainton

Of particular interest	Buckinghamshire Railway Centre,
	Quainton Tower Windmill
Accommodation	The White Hart (01296) 75234
	Village shop, Church St (01296) 75233
Refreshments	Two pubs
PO/village shops	Post office, village stores, small butcher's
Public phone	Yes
Bank	No
Parking	Roadside, around village green
	Car park available for visitors to Railway Centre
Access	Road N off A41(T) between Aylesbury and Bicester
	Rail Nearest station, Aylesbury (01494) 441561
	Bus (01296) 75234

QUAINTON - NORTH MARSTON - SWANBOURNE - (8 miles)

Of particular interest

Quainton Hill - spectacular views; North Marston - Medieval pilgrimage church, Medieval Holy Well; Swanbourne - church plaque, chancel floor, Manor House, half-timbered/thatched houses.

AN OXBRIDGE WALK

Quainton to Swanbourne
8 miles

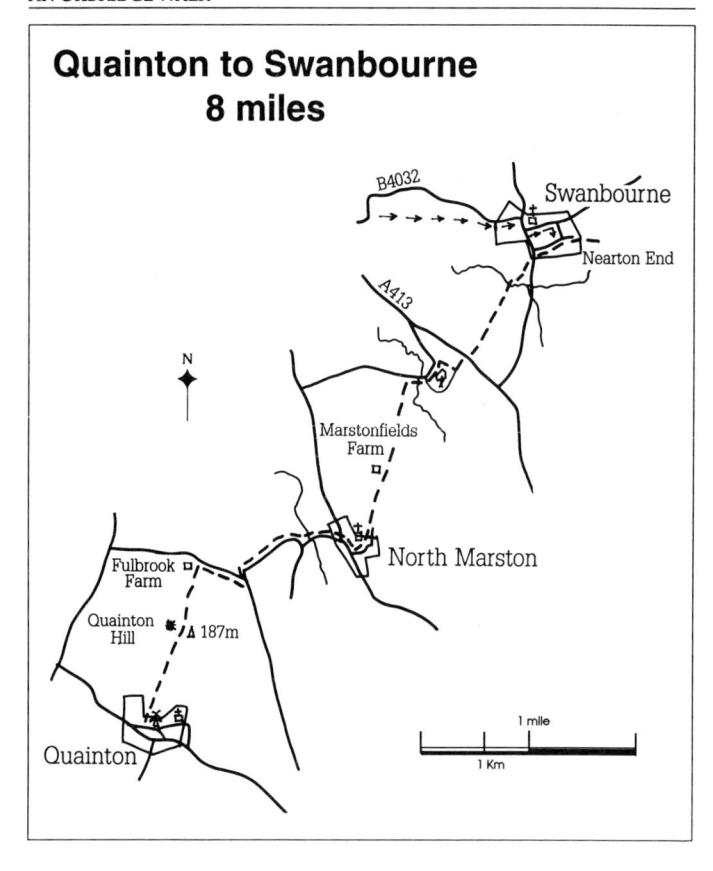

Map showing the route from Quainton through Quainton Hill, Fulbrook Farm, North Marston, Marstonfields Farm to Swanbourne and Nearton End, with roads A413 and B4032 marked.

The North Bucks/Midshires Way follows the road (Upper Street), from the top left-hand corner of the green, turning right at the waymarked finger-post up the side of a thatched, half-timbered house opposite the playing fields. The path, paved with old stone slabs, begins to climb almost immediately and reaches the lower slopes of Quainton Hill via a wooden swing gate. From here it continues ahead over another stile half-way up the hill aiming to the left of the mast on the summit.

Just below the summit the bumps and hollows of old stone workings provide an ideal resting place from which to enjoy the highest (187m) viewpoint on the Oxbridge Walk, with the Chiltern escarpment to the south and the distant Cotswolds to the north-west, beyond the brick chimneys.

The route continues over a stile in the right-hand corner of a hedge running across the line of march and, having passed the mast on the right, turns right, over another stile. The path then follows the hedge on the right up to a metal farm-gate to the rear of the mast, where it turns left along the ridge (Quainton Hill) to another metal gate in the hedge opposite.

The North Bucks Way and the Swan's Way converge from the gate at the rear of the mast down to the bottom of the hill.

Through the gate the path runs diagonally right down the hill keeping to the left of the mound topped by wooden windbreaks, and heading well to the right of a red-brick cattle-shed or barn at the bottom of the hill. It then goes over a wooden footbridge next to a gate and, keeping to the right of the electricity pole in the second field, the path meets a narrow, gated lane.

Two small villages once stood in the fields before the lane but were abandoned in medieval times. The main buildings of Fulbrook Farm, seen when descending the hill, are said to have been partly built with stone taken from the ruins.

The Oxbridge route now parts company with the North Bucks Way, as it turns right here to follow the lane and the Swan's/ Midshires Way. When the T junction is reached, the route turns left to follow a minor road across arable farmland for about a mile before arriving at the village of North Marston. Here it turns right to follow the main road for a few hundred yards as far as Manor Farm (B+B accommodation available), where it crosses over the road to The Bell pub. From the pub it turns right up School Hill for a short distance and then turns right again down the side of Yew Cottage on a path from which a gate leads into the churchyard.

North Marston is an extensive farming village with some attractive houses in the vicinity of the village church which, together with the Holy Well (still to be seen in Schorne Lane), was a popular place of pilgrimage in the Middle Ages. A cult grew around John Schorne, the Rector from 1290 to

1314, and pilgrims came from as far afield as Norfolk because of miracles said to have been worked here and at the Holy Well in the village. John Schorne was supposed to have "conjured the devil into a boot and the church once held a mechanical representation of the devil in his boot which may have been the original Jack (devil) in a Box (boot). Today, the names of various pubs in the area can be attributed to the legend, an obvious example being, The Devil in the Boot, Winslow. John Schorne's relics were carried off to St George's Chapel, Windsor Castle, in 1478 and at this time the present chancel was built - perhaps in an attempt to placate the villagers. The chancel was subsequently restored and the stained glass put in by Queen Victoria, in 1854, with part of the money left to her by a local miser and landowner.

From the church the route turns left to follow the Swan's/ Midshires Way along a narrow road once the old pilgrim's way from the north. At the end of a line of houses on the right, the road becomes the drive leading across arable fields to Marstonfields Farm.

A new, red-brick "Dallas-ranch" style building on the left-hand side of the drive, before Marstonfields Farm is reached, sticks out like a sore thumb from the surrounding countryside, but serves as an unmissable landmark!

At the end of the long drive is Marstonfields Farm where the route turns right via two metal gates, after which it heads diagonally left across a pasture to another gate set in the hedge. From here the path runs ahead over fields and through a series of gates before reaching a lane where the route turns right. At the second left-hand bend, the Swan's Way goes right, down a wide green, or drovers' road with a small wood (Christmas Gorse), ahead and to the right.

Where the route turns right, two cottages can be seen further along the lane which have been built on the site of an inn famous in its day for the "kick-shin" and bare-knuckle boxing contests staged in the field opposite. Quiet and peaceful today, history records that the green lanes and turnpike roads in this area of Buckinghamshire once thronged with crowds on their way to cheer on "Johnny Thunder", the local pugilistic hero!

The route follows the green lane to where the wood bars the way ahead, where it turns left up a track leading to the road at the top of the rise which it crosses straight over. On the other side a headland track leads down to a continuation of the green lane which runs straight ahead for almost a mile before reverting to a track leading to another road.

Here the Oxbridge route turns left along the road and, some distance up the rise ahead, leaves the Swan's/Midshires Way as it turns right into a narrow lane signposted "Nearton End Only".

Nearton End is part of the village of Swanbourne and a short distance down this lane the Cross Bucks Way comes in on the left down a path from the centre of the village. Arrival here marks a significant meeting of ways, as far as the Oxbridge route is concerned, since it is where the western half of the Cross Bucks Way (the northerly route from Oxford, via the Oxford Canal) joins this route, which left Oxford via the River Thames.

The route continues along Nearton Lane which is lined with attractive houses and estate cottages.

B+B accommodation is available at Brises Farm, a sixteenth century, half timbered Tudor Manor House, complete with herringbone brickwork and some original windows. The farmhouse is probably of monastic origins, a one time cell of the Prior of St Mary de Pre, St Albans. Opposite the Methodist Chapel stands the half-timbered farmhouse belonging to Brooks Farm, part of which is the surviving half of a medieval hall house. The west wall was once internal and is the best example of cruck building seen on the walk since Long Crendon. Further along on the left Hart House is passed which was once the White Hart, a pub which served the drovers who used this lane on the long journey to market.

At the end of Nearton Lane the route turns right along a track way-marked for the Cross Bucks Way which is followed from here to where it ends at Old Linslade on the Grand Union Canal.

GENERAL INFORMATION

En Route

Of particular interest	Quainton Hill -	spectacular views
	North Marston -	Medieval pilgrimage church
	-	Medieval holy well
Accommodation	North Marston -	Manor Farm (01296) 67252
Refreshments	North Marston -	one pub
PO/shop	North Marston -	antiques shop only
Public phone	North Marston	
Banks	None	
Parking	North Marston - roadside only	

Swanbourne

Of particular interest	Church (plaque on chancel floor)
	Manor House, half-timbered/thatched houses
Accommodation	Brises Farm, Nearton End (01296) 720214
	PO/village stores (01296) 720288
Refreshments	Cottage tea rooms (cream teas, coffee, lunches)
	Open 10am-5pm, Mon - Wed
	10am-6pm, Sat & Sun
PO/shop	Yes (inc.off-licence)
Public phone	Yes
Bank	No (nearest, Winslow)
Parking	Roadside only
Access	Road B4032 E of Winslow
	Rail Nearest station, Bletchley (Milton Keynes)
	Northampton Line (01908) 370883
	Bus (01296) 84919, (01908) 668366

SWANBOURNE - STEWKLEY - SOULBURY - LINSLADE - LEIGHTON BUZZARD (9 miles)

Of particular interest

Stewkley - Norman church; Soulbury - limestone grit boulder (glacial erratic); Old Linslade - disused church; Linslade/Leighton Buzzard - Grand Union Canal; Leighton Buzzard - All Saints church, narrow gauge railway.

At the end of Nearton Lane, the Cross Bucks Way turns right along a way-marked track past "The Barn".

Within a short distance, what starts as a headland path becomes a green or drovers' road once more along which stock was driven to the meat markets in London from as far away as the Welsh borders. The track is well defined and easy to follow for the next mile or so, but care should be taken as it is deeply rutted and uneven in places.

The hedged-in track continues ahead, generally in an easterly direction. Later, it becomes a headland track keeping to the left of the hedge along the bottom of wide, arable fields. Eventually (ignoring the new footbridge on the right), the track reaches the

THAME TO LEIGHTON BUZZARD

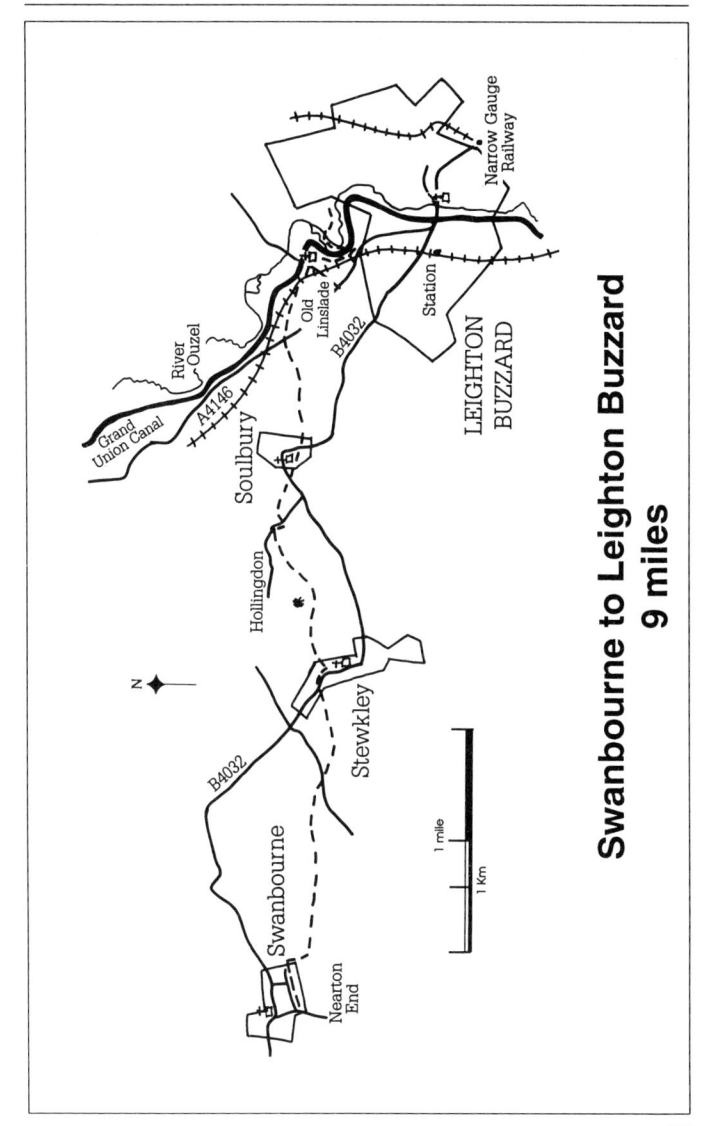

Swanbourne to Leighton Buzzard
9 miles

corner of the field ahead where it is reduced to a narrow, overgrown footpath through scrubby woodland, an attractive habitat for butterflies in summer months.

After a few hundred yards the path turns right, over an inconspicuous stile just beyond a larger oak tree, and then left, to follow the line of the hedge up to the top corner of the field. Here, a stile leads to a T junction of tracks. The route follows the track opposite (with the way-marked oak-post in the middle) for a few yards and then turns right through the hedge and over a ditch and stile. From here the path crosses a wide pasture heading to the right of the farm buildings up rising ground giving open views to the north, with Mursley water tower clearly visible to the north-west. After a double stile the path heads for another in the left-hand corner of the field in front. From here it turns right down a narrow pasture, past a recently cleared pond, to a stile in the left-hand corner. A few yards along the drive to Lower Dean Farm, the route turns left along Dean Road. After a short distance along the road it turns right for a hundred yards or so along a concrete track leading to Dean Tithe Farm.

The hamlet of Stewkley Dean, long abandoned, was once sited in the fields here. No trace of the hamlet remains above ground but it is commemorated in the name of the road and farms in the vicinity.

The route leaves the farm track on the left at the circular walk sign, and follows the hedge to the corner of the field. From here (ignoring the stile to the left) it turns right over a double stile and footbridge, keeping to the right of the hedge in the next field for about 20 yards. The route then turns left over another double stile and footbridge and heads diagonally right across a field to more stiles and a footbridge in the bottom left-hand corner. The path again follows the hedge and, about half-way across the bottom of the field, turns right to the other side of the hedge via yet more stiles and a footbridge. From here it turns left along the line of the hedge and carries on ahead, back on the course of the old drovers' road, over a series of stiles and then through a metal gate. A short track from here leads to a road in the village of Stewkley where the route crosses to the roadside path on the other side and turns right.

Stewkley is built on a north-west ridge of high ground and has some interesting sixteenth- and seventeenth-century timber-framed houses and cottages along its mile-long High Street. Built with north and south "Ends", the village has the second of two splendid Norman churches along the Oxbridge route (the first being the church at Iffley in Oxfordshire). St Michael's church, built about 1150, is described by Pevsner as "The most spendid piece of Norman parochial architecture in Buckinghamshire, and in addition exceptionally complete and unaltered". Having escaped Victorian "improvements" and survived its earlier use as a stables by Parliamentary Cavalry in the Civil War, the church came closest to meeting its end in more recent times, when the entire village of Stewkley mobilised to fight a successful campaign to avoid being razed to the ground as the site of London's Third Airport.

If visiting the church, follow the road past the village post office and general stores. There are pubs for refreshment, but no B+B accommodation available in the village.

Having turned right along the roadside path, the route passes a garage on the left and, a few hundred yards further along on the same side (before the village PO/shop is reached), the Cross Bucks Way turns left at a way-marked finger-post. From here the route goes over a stile at the end of a short track and across the field in front to where a plank over a ditch leads to another stile. The path then follows the hedge for the next two fields to a stile and footbridge closely followed by another stile at the top of a bank. From here it crosses two more fields to a stile next to a gate where the path leads down into and across the bottom of a small valley. At the bottom of the long rise another stile leads to a headland path which follows the hedge uphill.

Almost at the top of the hill, on the left-hand side of the path, is a memorial seat with good views to the north. In the far distance is Milton Keynes, Britain's first new city, with a planned population of 250,000 by the end of the century.

The path continues to keep to the right of the hedge up to the corner of the second field where the line of the route is indicated for the first time by a large white arrow in addition to the usual way-marking (courtesy of the Chiltern Ramblers). From here the path runs downhill over open sheep pastures, keeping to the left of a clump of willows on the other side of the second field where a stile takes the path to the left of a wire fence. After about a hundred yards the path switches to the other side of the fence via a stile and bears left down a small valley. It then turns right down a bank next to a large sycamore tree and follows the path past some farm buildings where the route turns right along the lane in the hamlet of Hollingdon.

From the sycamore tree onwards, the quality of the path is poor since it is invariably overgrown with stinging nettles which makes it difficult to follow in places. However, this stretch only lasts for about a hundred yards.

Having turned right from the path, the route follows the lane down a hill before turning left at a way-marked finger-post. The path then crosses a small pasture and a footbridge over a stream before climbing a small hill keeping to the left of an excavation. From a stile in the fence the path continues to the top of the hill where it runs through a farmyard between a thatched farmhouse and fenced-in horse jumps. Over another stile the path runs along the right-hand side of the back garden of a house to emerge on a narrow lane.

The route crosses the lane and, via an iron swing-gate, heads diagonally left to the top left-hand corner of the field in front, to a stile next to a road. From a metal gate across the road to the left, the path runs downhill, diagonally right, skirting the cricket pitch. It then turns left through a gate and the churchyard of All Saints, Soulbury.

Soulbury's church contains monuments to the Lovett family, one-time Lords of the Manor who lived in the extensive Liscombe Park estate to the south. One of the monuments, to Robert Lovett who died in 1690, is in white marble and thought to be the work of Grinling Gibbons. In addition to the church, the village has some pleasant cottages and one curiousity, a millstone grit boulder left here by the retreating glaciers at the end of the ice age. In the past, superstitious stories about the stone included one that it rolls down the hill and back up again when the clock in the nearby church strikes midnight, although the fact that the village pub is at the bottom of the hill in question might have had something to do with this particular story!

Turn left up the road to see the glacial erratic, or right for The Boot pub. There is no B+B available in the village.

The Cross Bucks Way carries straight over the road and down

a narrow lane at the bottom of which it turns right through a swing-gate. From here a wide track runs down the field to a stile where the path turns left. It then runs over a long pasture, first passing in front of an Anglia Water pumping station before heading diagonally right, almost to the bottom corner of the field. On the other side of a footbridge the path continues ahead over a small field to a stile from where it heads diagonally left across two large, arable fields. From the stile on the far side of the second field, the path continues in roughly the same direction, clipping the bottom corner of the next field and heading to the right of a clump of pines in the hedge-line. From a gateway gap in the hedge the path runs uphill (with Chelmscote Manor Farm, a sixteenth-century manor house on the left), to a large storage tank, where the route turns right along a track. After a hundred yards or so it turns left over a wooden fence, to follow a path which runs just inside the edge of a plantation of young trees. On the other side of the plantation, the route crosses to the left, over the main A4146. This is a very busy road and the crossing point is quite dangerous due to the difficulty of anticipating traffic coming from the right.

The route runs down the bank from the road to a stile. From here it heads diagonally right across a rough pasture to another stile on the other side of which it continues up to the brow of the hill ahead. From the hill the path carries on in the same direction, aiming to the right of the white house below, from where it continues ahead keeping to the right of the hedge. It then crosses a drive and a stile followed by undulating pastures, heading to the left of a large oak tree. Having passed the tree, the path crosses a footbridge over the main railway line. On the other side of the bridge, the Grand Union Canal can be seen in the field below and the route heads to the right, keeping to the left-hand side of the large mound in front.

With the canal on the left, the path continues ahead over a wide pasture to where it meets the road just above a bridge over the canal. Here the route first turns right to follow the road and then turns left at a way-marked finger-post through the extended churchyard of St Mary's church.

(St Mary's Church, Old Linslade, has seen better days and is disused except for special occasions. Now on the Bedfordshire side of the border, it

was once deemed to be one of the richest churches in Buckinghamshire.)

From the churchyard, the path runs behind Old Linslade Manor House and down to the canal where the route turns right to follow the canal for about half a mile to Bridge No 111, next to the Globe Inn, where the Cross Bucks Way ends.

On the other side of the bridge, the Oxbridge route continues along the Greensand Ridgeway across the county of Bedfordshire. However, B+B accommodation is available a mile to the south along the canal tow-path, in the market town of Leighton Buzzard.

Leighton Buzzard is a town of Saxon origins with a late fourteenth- or early fifteenth-century cross still standing at the top end of its market square. The town's importance increased in the days when it lay on the main coaching route between Oxford and Cambridge and the Swan hotel in the High Street survives as a fine example of a coaching inn from this era.

All Saints Church is a large ironstone church particularly notable for its pinnacled tower and broach spire rising to 191ft. The church has an interesting interior inlcuding the famous "Kempe" windows and an original font that has been in use for more than seven hundred years!

Leighton Buzzard Narrow Gauge Railway, known as "England's Friendly Little Line", operates rare steam and diesel engines. Originally built to serve the sand quarries a few miles away, the line has been restored and the locomotives now pull passenger trains on various days of the week Mar-Oct.

For further information contact Page's Park Station (01525) 373888.

GENERAL INFORMATION

En Route

Of particular interest	Stewkley - Norman church
	Soulbury - limestone grit boulder (glacial erratic)
	Old Linslade - disused church
	Linslade/Leighton Buzzard - Grand Union Canal
Accommodation	None
Refreshments	Stewkley - three pubs
	Soulbury - one pub/restaurant
PO/shops	Stewkley

Public phones	Stewkley, Soulbury
Banks	None
Parking	Stewkley - limited, roadside
	Soulbury - limited roadside

Leighton Buzzard

Of particular interest	All Saints church,
	Narrow gauge railway
Accommodation	Park View Hotel (nr station) (01525) 374692
	The Black Horse, North St (01525) 381129
	Grovebury Farm (road to Aylesbury) (01525) 373363
	Heath Park House (road to Woburn) (01525) 381646
Refreshments	Pubs, restaurants, cafes
PO/shops etc	Main post office, many shops, supermarkets
Outdoor eqpt	Bargain Clothing Stores (01525) 374752
	Millets (01525) 371623
Public phones	Yes
Banks	Yes
Car parks	Multi-storey, West St
	Hockliffe St, Church Square, North St, railway station
Market days	Tues, Sat
Tourist information	Library, Lake St (01525) 371788
Access	Road A418 (Aylesbury to Bedford, links A5 & M1)
	Rail Leighton Buzzard (Linslade) Station,
	London (Euston) to Rugby line (01908) 370883
	Bus (01234) 228337

AN OXBRIDGE WALK

BEDFORDSHIRE
LEIGHTON BUZZARD - GAMLINGAY

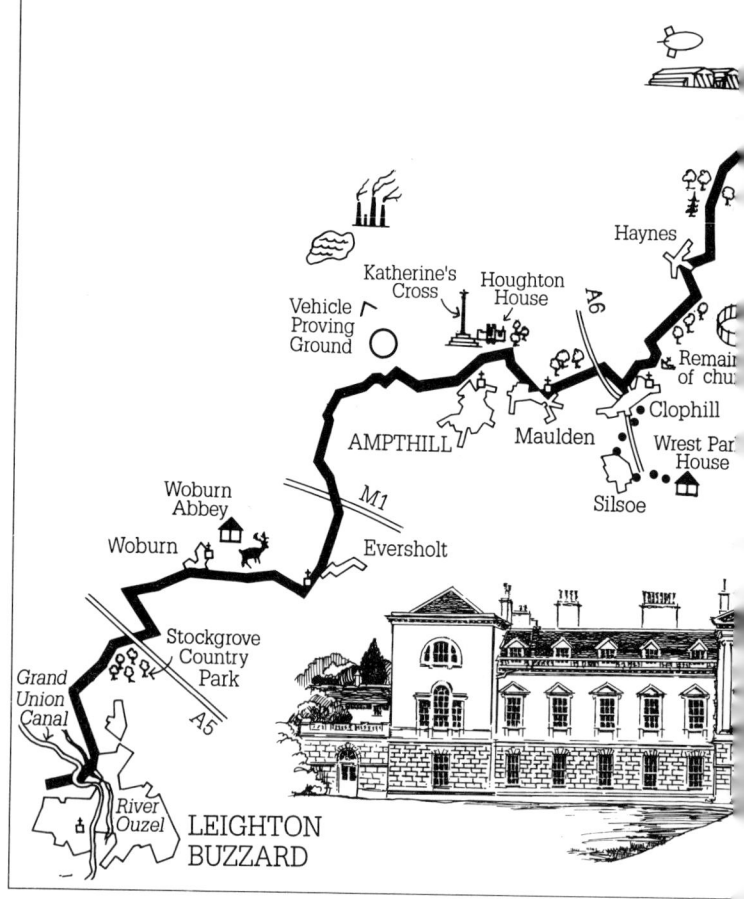

Haynes

Katherine's Cross
Houghton House
Vehicle Proving Ground
A6
Remains of chu...
Clophill
AMPTHILL
Maulden
Wrest Park House
Silsoe

Woburn Abbey
M1
Woburn
Eversholt

Stockgrove Country Park
A5
Grand Union Canal

River Ouzel
LEIGHTON BUZZARD

64

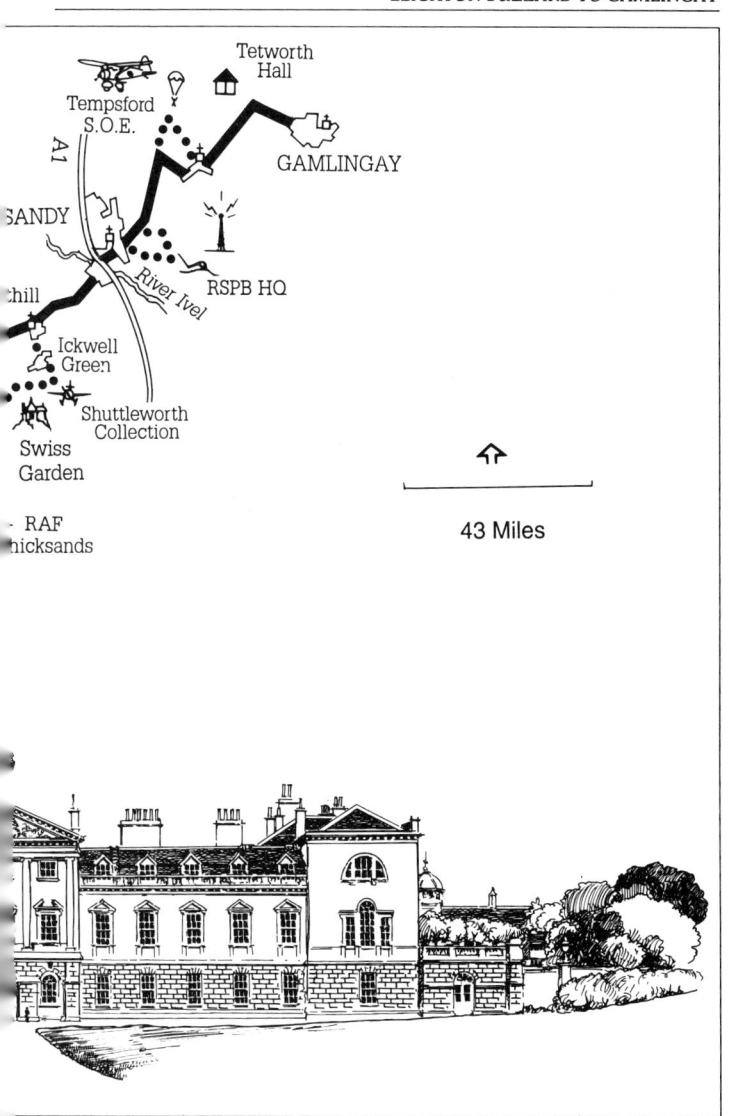

LEIGHTON BUZZARD TO GAMLINGAY

Tetworth Hall
Tempsford S.O.E.
A1
GAMLINGAY
SANDY
River Ivel
RSPB HQ
chill
Ickwell Green
Shuttleworth Collection
Swiss Garden
RAF Chicksands

43 Miles

Leighton Buzzard to Gamlingay: 43 miles

LEIGHTON BUZZARD - WOBURN - (8 miles)

Of particular interest

Stockgrove Country Park; Woburn Abbey and Park; Woburn Safari Park (cars only); Woburn Village Heritage Centre.

From the end of the Cross Bucks Way, the route crosses the bridge over the Grand Union Canal to the stile on the other side just before the road turns right.

This stile marks the start of the Greensand Ridge Walk (GRW) which runs west-east from here across Bedfordshire. Within sight of the bridge is the Globe Inn, a very pleasant pub complete with canalside gardens. The market town of Leighton Buzzard is about a mile to the south along the canal tow-path from here.

In crossing the canal, the Oxbridge route also crosses the newly created Grand Union Canal Walk and joins the start of the Two Ridges Link path with the Ridgeway National Trail.

From the stile, with the canal immediately on the left, the path keeps to the right of the hedge as far as a way-marked oak-post where it heads diagonally right across open pastures to turn left along the bank of the River Ouzel.

The river divided Leighton Buzzard from Linslade before they were made one town in 1966, and once marked the boundary here between Bedfordshire and Buckinghamshire.

After a few hundred yards along the river bank the route turns right over a substantial wooden footbridge on the other side of which it continues up the hill in front before turning left along a metalled track.

There are good views from here across the Ouzel valley and in the middle foreground can be seen the old church of St Mary's, which the Oxbridge route passed close by on the last stage of the Cross Bucks Way.

The route follows the track until it crosses a cattle grid, where it turns left along a sandy track at the base of the ridge with the river

Leighton Buzzard to Woburn
8 miles

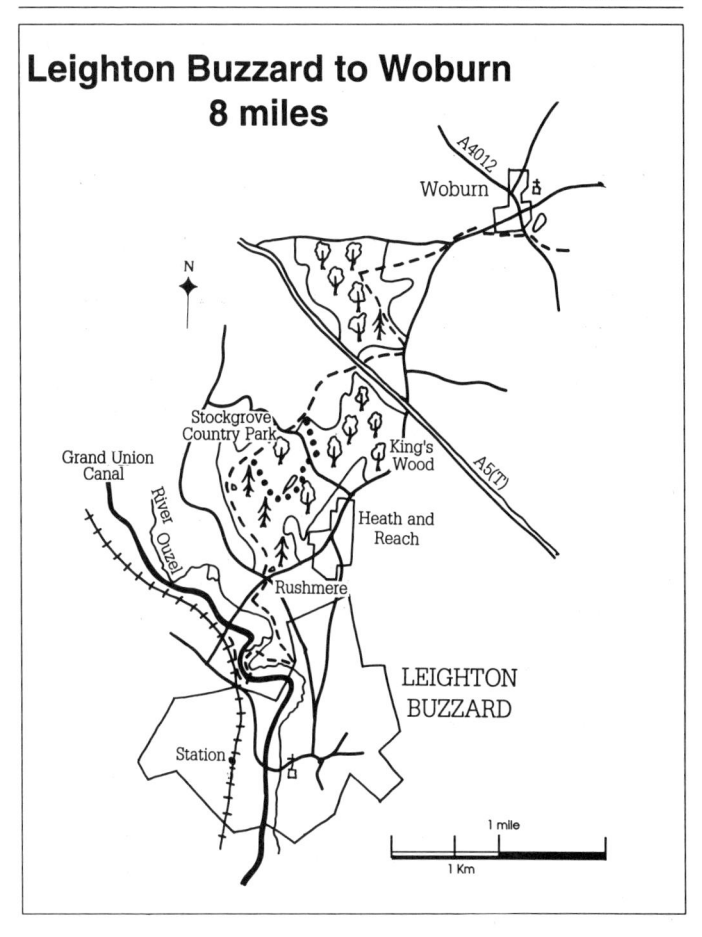

Ouzel on the left. The track goes to the right of a metal gate and, after passing through the second of two wooden swing-gates, turns immediately right off the main track and bears left up to the top of this spur of the ridge. From here it turns right to run downhill along the edge of the woods with further fine views across the valley. Just before reaching the road ahead the path turns right and runs

67

through the beechwoods parallel to the road before leading down to a crossroads. Here the route takes the road opposite, with the gates of Rushmore Park to the right.

These gates were originally the entrance to what is now Stockgrove Country Park. The entrance lodges and gates, like most of the buildings at Stockgrove Park, were designed by William Curtis Green RA, and built in the 1930s.

About 50 yards along the road, the GRW turns right to enter the woods at a way-marked finger-post. From here the path skirts giant red-woods planted on the edge of a lake before bearing left, following way-marked oak-posts up to the crest of the ridge along which it turns right.

The sandy path now runs alongside plantations of conifers on the right. Notice the tiny swing-gates set at intervals in the wire-netting fences which protect the nursery tree plantations from bark stripping by deer. These gates open when pushed by smaller animals and allow access to through routes and long-used runs.

The path continues straight ahead, along the ridge, until reaching a stile with a notice which indicates the limit of the woods bordering Stockgrove Country Park. Over the stile the track keeps to the left of a small pond before running uphill to a T junction, where the route turns right. The track continues in the same direction, ignoring tracks to left and right, until arriving at cross-tracks in a cleared area.

At this point there is an opportunity to include in the route a visit to Stockgrove Country park, a designated SSSI complete with visitors' centre. Those walkers who wish to stay on the GRW should continue straight ahead, over the cross-tracks. Those choosing to visit the park should turn down the track on the right, way-marked by an oak finger-post indicating that the park lies half a mile from here. This involves a detour of a mile and a half, but only adds about a mile to the overall length of this stage as the GRW is rejoined further along the main route. Those who do not wish to take this detour should continue with the section marked "Main Route" below, which stays with the GRW.

Recommended Detour - Stockgrove Country Park

After turning right from the cross-tracks, the path runs downhill and forks left at a concrete hard standing. It then passes the Dower House on the left, which originally provided temporary accommodation whilst the nearby neo-Georgian mansion was being built.

The mansion is now Stockgrove Park School and is not part of the Park.

The path keeps to the left at the next oak finger-post and runs through a woodland area of Scots pine mixed with rhododendrons before descending the hill. Half way down the hill a newly built, wooden swing-gate marks the boundary of the Park. At the bottom of the hill the route turns left, in front of a wooden seat, to follow a broad track along the edge of Baker's Wood which, together with nearby 'King's Wood', forms the largest block of deciduous woodland in Bedfordshire.

Stockgrove Country Park's 74 acres are managed jointly by Bedfordshire and Buckinghamshire County Council. The park has an exceptional range of soil types which support a rich variety of species and habitats. Some areas of heathland survive which support Greensand indicator species such as heather, gorse and broom. However, most of this area has been woodland for many centuries and King's Wood gets its name from the thirteenth century, when it was part of the medieval Royal Manor of Leighton Buzzard. Apart from deer, the woods here, and where they exist along the rest of the Greensand Ridge, also contain many of the county's more interesting bird species, including woodpeckers, nuthatches, tree pipits, redstarts, woodwarblers, woodcocks and Lady Amherst's pheasant.

The track continues ahead and eventually forks round both sides of a large lake which provides a haven for water-fowl.

The right-hand fork leads to a lakeside seat supported at each end by stone representations of the Kroyer Kielberg family's coat of arms, the family that once owned all this park and its mansion. The coat of arms once graced the main entrance to the Park and a close study soon reveals the family's Danish origins and maritime connections.

From the lake a broad track carries on to the main entrance to Stockgrove Country Park where there is a car park, toilets, visitors' centre, refreshments and picnic areas.

The park is open all the year round and admission is free.

The visitors' centre is open Apr-September, Tues-Sat, 1pm-4.30pm, Sun and Bank Hol, 12-6pm. In the winter, Oct-Mar, 12-4pm.

After the visitors' centre, the route crosses the road, which at this point marks the boundary between the counties of Bedfordshire and Buckinghamshire. From the stile opposite, the path bears left up the line of a shallow valley. It then carries on ahead over a series of stiles until, just after crossing a track preceded by a sign warning of heavy lorries, a final stile marks the point where the detour rejoins the GRW.

Main Route

From the cross-tracks the GRW continues ahead along a broad, sandy track which eventually emerges from the woods and passes through the remains of what was once a large country estate.

Stockgrove House with its distinctive Clock Tower is passed on the right. This neo-Georgian building was built in the 1920s and together with what were once stable blocks has been converted into private residences. Notice on the left, just after passing Oakwood cottages, a large walled garden complete with elaborate wrought-iron gates incorporating the initials of a previous owner. With the break-up of the family estates the gardens, which originally kept five gardeners busy, were abandoned and at one time became so overgrown as to be almost forgotten.

A few hundred yards further on, the track meets the road, next to the North Lodge of Stockgrove Park School. Here the route turns right to follow the road for a short distance before the GRW turns left at a way-marked finger-post next to a lay-by. From here a sandy track follows the edge of wide pastures across which can be seen the whitewashed and thatched buildings of Cherry Orchard farm. The route then crosses the line of another track running from left to right, which is also where the **detour rejoins the main route**.

The route dog-legs across the track in front, first left along the line of the track and then leaving it on the right. From here it continues ahead until a stile is reached on the edge of woodland which has been virtually continuous since leaving Leighton Buzzard. The path runs over the small pasture ahead and turns right along the fence up the side of Rammamere Farm to a stile in the corner of the field. Over the stile the path keeps to the right of the hedge up a large, open pasture to the stile in the top left-hand corner where it turns left. Two stiles later the route descends via steep steps and crosses diagonally right over the main A5(Watling Street).

A long while ago, the woods extended up to and beyond this road.

However, the Statute of Winchester, 1285, required that all woods bordering highways between market towns should be cleared back to a distance of 200ft in order to deprive footpads and highwaymen of the cover from which they ambushed unfortunate travellers. This road (originally a Roman road) has always held dangers for travellers. In the past it was highwaymen, "gentlemen of the road" such as Black Tom and Dick Turpin; today, it is Heavy Goods Vehicles.

After negotiating the road and the steps in the opposite embankment, the GRW is signposted across two arable fields on the other side of which it meets a minor road. Here the route turns left and follows the road for about a hundred yards before turning left along a way-marked bridleway.

This track eventually enters woodlands in which deer are a common sight due to the proximity of Woburn Deer Park from which they originally escaped. This particular section of the route can be wet and muddy in places at any time of the year.

The track continues straight ahead for about a quarter of a mile before turning right at a way-marked cross-tracks in the middle of the woods. From here the track continues through woodland for a few hundred yards and then emerges to run across arable farmland and past a white, thatched farmhouse, shortly after which it meets a road. Here the route turns left continuing along the road and up the rise to where the GRW turns right through an iron farm-gate opposite Maryland College. It then follows the track over the hill and and continues down the left-hand side of a broad avenue of trees with Woburn Abbey ahead. After a few hundred yards, the route turns left through a belt of trees and across a small pasture to reach the road leading into the village of Woburn.

This village with its attractive Georgian houses is approximately half way along the route between Oxford and Cambridge and is, therefore, a natural stopping-off point. Turn left along the road for the village or right if continuing along the route.

Woburn contains many fine examples of Georgian architecture and together with the nearby Abbey and Safari Park is one of Bedford's best known tourist attractions. The village reached the height of its prosperity and importance in the mid-nineteenth century when it served as an important staging post on the Oxford-Cambridge route. Some of the coaching inns have survived together with the old (although not original) town hall, the old grammar school in Bedford Street and the tower of the original St Mary's church, to which was subsequently added a mortuary chapel. This latter building serves as a Heritage and Tourist Information Centre and is well worth a visit for those interested in discovering more about Woburn and its history. The ground floor of the old town hall has been converted into an antiques centre, but the school, built in 1582, still serves the village in its original capacity and must have one of the longest records of continuous use in the county.

The "new" St Mary's church, completed in 1868 by William, 8th Duke of Bedford is in Park Street opposite what is now a car park. A grand Victorian church, it was built with a large crypt intended as the final resting place for succeeding generations of the Russell family. The Duke was fond of showing visitors the hole in the floor through which he was to be lowered after his death, to the sound of solemn music. However, the crypt remains empty to this day as the family prefers to be buried in the Bedford Chapel of Chenies Parish Church, in Buckinghamshire, where the family originated. The spire of the church was dismantled in 1892 due to its dangerous condition and the square tower is now surmounted by three sinister looking grotesques that glare balefully down at passing parishioners.

Woburn Abbey has been the home of the Dukes of Bedford for over 350 years and is built on the site of a Cistercian Monastery dating back to 1145. The Abbey and much of its surrounding parkland is open to the public. The house contains an impressive private collection of paintings, furniture, porcelain and silver. The 3000 acres of parkland, landscaped by Humphrey Repton in the nineteenth century, contains many rare trees, including the largest known tree in Bedfordshire, and provides the home for over 1000 deer. The herds contain nine different species of deer, one of which, the Milu or Pere David, was preserved from extinction at Woburn. During the summer season, the Flying Duchess Pavilion Coffee Shop serves hot and cold food and beverages. There are also extensive designated picnic areas within the Park. For further details (admission charges etc.) (01525) 290666.

Woburn Safari Park is available to motorists only. (01525) 290407)

GENERAL INFORMATION

En Route

Of particular interest	Stockgrove Country Park
Accommodation	Heath and Reach (Stockgrove Country Park)
	Rose Cottage, Brickhill Rd (01525) 237885
	Heath and Reach - Cockhorse Hotel
	(take Brickhill Rd to A418) (01525) 23390
Refreshments	Grand Union Canal - The Globe Inn
	Stockgrove Country Park - snack bar, summer afternoons only
PO/shops	None
Public phone	None
Banks	None - nearest, Leighton Buzzard
Parking	Stockgrove Country Park - free car park

Woburn

Of particular interest	Woburn Abbey and Park
	Woburn Safari Park (cars only)
	Heritage Centre and Georgian houses
Accommodation	'Copperfield' tea rooms & guest house (01525) 290464
	The Magpie pub (01525) 290219
	11 George St (01525) 290405
Camping	Ridgmont - Rose and Crown (01525) 280245
	(1 mile E on A4012 Crawley Rd)
Refreshments	Five pubs, two hotels, tearooms, restaurants
PO/shops	Post office, village stores, gift shops
Outdoor eqpt	Tony Wild Camping (01525) 290477
Public phone	Yes
Banks	None - nearest, Woburn Sands, 2 miles
Parking	Large, free car park, Park Street
Tourist information	Heritage Centre - Old St Mary's church
Misc	Heated, open-air swimming pool
	(opp. village hall at northern end of village)
Access	Road M1 (Junction 13)
	A5(T) between Dunstable and Milton Keynes
	Rail Aspley Guise or Woburn Sands Station
	(Bedford to Bletchley Branch line) (01908) 370883
	Bus (01234) 228337

WOBURN - EVERSHOLT - MILLBROOK - AMPTHILL -
(11 miles)

Of particular interest
Woburn Abbey and Deer Park; Vehicle Proving Ground - views; Ampthill - St Katherine's Cross, Georgian houses, coaching inns.

At the road into Woburn, the Greensand Ridge Walk (GRW) turns right for a few hundred yards as far as Ivy Lodge on the left-hand side. To the left of the lodge a way-marked path continues to follow the line of Wayne Close as it approaches the Deer Park and the West Face of Woburn Abbey. From an iron swing-gate the route bears to the left following way-marked oak posts at intervals across open parkland, passing between lakes across the right-hand one of which there is a good view of the impressive west face of Woburn Abbey.

In front of the Abbey, on the other side of the lake, stands the equine statue of "Mrs Moss", a memorial and tribute to a celebrated horse from the Abbey's stud which produced 15 foals, ten of which were winners of important races.

Across the park to the left is the landing ground originally used by the Flying Duchess and still in use for the annual fly-in of the de Havilland Moth Club.

Past the right-hand lake, the route crosses a road and bears diagonally right up to the top of the hill from where it runs past the main visitors' entrance to the Abbey on the right and the car park on the left.

From the top of the hill there are good views across the park to the village of Woburn and over the surrounding countryside.

"Mrs Moss"

Woburn to Ampthill
11 miles

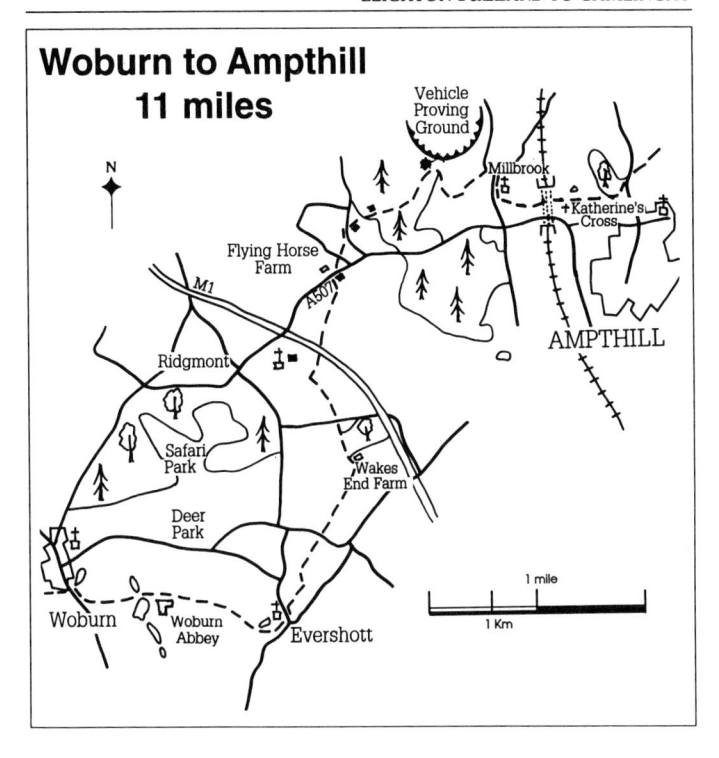

Map showing route from Woburn to Ampthill, featuring Vehicle Proving Ground, Millbrook, Katherine's Cross, Flying Horse Farm, Ridgmont, Ampthill, Safari Park, Wakes End Farm, Deer Park, Woburn, Woburn Abbey, and Evershott. M1 and A507 roads marked. Scale: 1 mile / 1 Km.

The route continues along the road past a vehicle barrier and, after a few hundred yards where the road bears right, the route follows ahead slightly to the left (east), along the line of more way-marked oak-posts. The path finally leaves the enclosed area of the Park via an elaborate wooden gate and stile, from where it continues down the hill through a fir-tree plantation and across a large, arable field. At the bottom of the field it crosses two streams feeding nearby Linden Lake and, from an oak finger-post, travels diagonally left across an open pasture to another footbridge over a stream. From here the path crosses a second pasture and goes through an iron swing-gate where the route turns left along the road into the village of Eversholt.

Eversholt has some attractive cottages clustered around a church and pub overlooking the village green - the sort of place that English "expats" dream of when feeling homesick. As with Swanbourne, the village through which the route travelled in Buckinghamshire, Eversholt consists of a number of "Ends", the most memorable, as far as the name is concerned, being Witts End.

The oldest parts of the church of St John the Baptist date back to the twelfth century, but most of it was built in the following three centuries. Sir Gilbert Scott, famous as the architect of St Pancras Station, was responsible for the over-restoration of the church in 1864. A local man, Edward Aveling Green, undertook much refurbishment of the interior.

The route follows the road past the church and The Green Man to where, as the road bends to the left, the GRW turns right along Brook End, a short cul-de-sac. About 50 yards past the last house on the right, the route turns left over a wooden footbridge crossing a shallow stream. From here the path turns right to follow the line of the hedge with the stream on the right. At a stile in the corner of the second field, the route turns left along a wide track or green lane similar to the drovers' track followed in Buckinghamshire. The route stays with the track, ignoring circular walk signs coming in from the right and left, and eventually crosses straight over the road at New Water End, past a row of typical turn of the century Bedford Estates cottages.

From here, the route continues along the way-marked track up and over the hill in front and past farm buildings on the left. Further along, the track passes through Briar Stockings Wood which straddles a Greensand outcrop, as indicated by the presence of gorse, broom and fir trees on the right. The path eventually emerges through a gateway on the other side of this wooded area to turn left on a headland path along the edge of the wood. After passing a pond on the left, the path passes through two iron gates and bears left behind Wakes Farm. Past the farm buildings it turns right on a track down the left hand side of Birchall's Wood heading for the distant road at the bottom of this wide valley.

After crossing the road (Cobblers Lane) the track carries straight on up the hill at the top of which there are good views across the valley to the south, whilst to the north-west can be seen the distant tower of the ruined church of Segenhoe Manor. The path continues ahead, keeping to the right of the hedge-line and then a small wood.

Just inside the wood can be seen the remains of a moat, further evidence of abandoned sites in this area.

At the end corner of the wood, a fence has to be negotiated, on the other side of which the route turns at right angles to follow the hedge along to a stile in the corner of a the field. From here the path runs to the left through a small copse and, via another stile, across a pasture to a bridge over the M1 motorway.

Over the bridge the GRW continues ahead across wide, arable fields, following a line of saplings down to the road to Manor Farm across which a headland path runs down the side of a very wide arable field. In the bottom corner of the field the route turns left over a footbridge across a deep stream. From here the path bears right and then left before going over a stile and skirting the left-hand edge of a storage area for agricultural machinery to where it meets the main A507. Here, it turns right for a hundred yards or so.

On the other side of the road, just before the GRW turns left, is Flying Horse Farm which was once another important staging post on the Oxford to Cambridge route. Its other claim to past fame is that the most famous highwayman of them all, Dick Turpin, is said to have spent the night here. Almost opposite Flying Horse Farm, Turnpike Cottage marks where the turnpike gate was once sited on this road.

The GRW leaves the road via a way-marked finger-post opposite Turnpike Cottage, heading diagonally right across an arable field. On the other side of the field a small lane is crossed and the route runs uphill keeping to the right of a belt of fir trees at the end of which the path crosses a short stretch of field before meeting another lane at the top of the hill. Here the route turns left for about a hundred yards before turning right on a way-marked track past a wide variety of free-range animals, including Vietnamese pot-bellied pigs, and the farm shop and campsite belonging to South View Farm.

The track continues ahead at a junction, after which it goes through the white gates of Jackdaw Hill House and continues past the front of the house and through a white gate opposite. From here the route follows a broad track through the ancient woodlands of Jackdaw Hill along the line of the ridge. When a small pond on the right is reached, the route first bears right, following the edge of the pond, and then turns left on a track along the boundary of a golf course. Eventually, the path reaches more open high ground where benches provide an ideal picnic spot from which there are splendid views over Marston Vale.

Plans exist to transform the view of this all too obviously man-made landscape over the next 30 years with the creation of a new community forest. In the foreground is the steeply banked circuit of the vehicle proving ground, whilst prominent in the middle distance are the tall chimneys of Stewartby brickworks - once the largest brickworks in the world and capable of producing around 650 million bricks a year. Close to the brickworks is a huge, disused clay pit, now the largest expanse of water in Bedfordshire, around which is centred Stewartby Country Park. The flooded clay pits in this area attract many interesting birds, vagrants and regular migrants; whilst gull roosts and water-fowl are particular features in winter. To the north-west, the county town of Bedford and its more obvious buildings can be picked out, whilst to the right of the town the landscape is dominated by the twin hulks of the massive airship sheds at Cardington.

On and around the picnic site, Bedford Ramblers' Club have planted 50 trees, one for each year since the club was formed.

From the picnic site, the path follows the chainlink fence marking the boundary of the vehicle proving grounds, and descends a flight of steep steps leading down off the ridge. At the bottom of the steps the path turns left and continues to follow the fence for some distance. Eventually the path leaves the fence just before a small car park is reached next to the road into Millbrook. Here the route turns right, up the short hill, and then right again along the road past the entrance to the golf club on the right and the Chequers pub on the left.

To the rear of the pub is a small camp site.

After passing the pub, the route continues along the road and up the hill until, just past the village hall on the left, the GRW follows a way-marked sunken path uphill to Millbrook parish church.

The location of the church of St Michael and all Angels, set somewhat apart from the village and on the brow of a hill, makes for an exceptionally peaceful setting. The top of the tower is 360ft above sea level and it is said that from here, with good visibility, it is possible to see the Wash! The churchyard contains a number of interesting headstones.

Gravestone, Millbrook churchyard

The route continues ahead before going straight over a crosstracks to follow a path between wire fences behind a line of farm buildings and a kennels. After passing a pond on the right, the path bends left and then turns right over a stile and into a small wood. On the other side of the wood it crosses a narrow pasture on the top of the main-line railway tunnel, and enters Ampthill park via a footbridge and a stile.

From here the route follows the usual GRW way-marked oak-posts past the occasional Scots pine to the top of the hill on which stand two commemorative stone crosses.

Katherine's Cross, the nearest of the two, was erected in 1773 to mark the site of the castle where Henry VIII imprisoned one of his six wives, Katherine of Aragon, during her trial and subsequent divorce. Most recently (1982) the cross made the national press as the place where a countrywide treasure hunt, instigated by Kit Williams in his book Masquerade, *ended with the unearthing of the final clue, a valuable gold necklace and jewelled hare.*

There are good views across the surrounding countryside on both sides of the ridge and, just past Katherine's Cross, a view-board depicts what can be seen in the landscape to the north. The second cross, further along the ridge top, is a memorial to those men from Ampthill who died in the First World War. It also marks the site of a military training camp established within the Park by the then Duke of Bedford.

The route continues past the second cross to where the track forks left for the GRW and right, down the hill for the market town of Ampthill. The left-hand fork leads to a wooden swing-gate and a path through a wood from which it emerges on the road almost at the top of the hill out of Ampthill (in all probability, "Hill Difficulty" in John Bunyan's *Pilgrim's Progress*.

At this point the GRW turns left, up the hill, on the roadside path.

Here there is also a second chance to turn right, down the hill and into Ampthill.

Ampthill is a historic town with many listed Georgian buildings, the fronts of which often conceal even older interiors. A market has been held in the town on a Thursday every year since 1219 and the combined town pump and milestone to one side of the crossroads in the centre of the town stands in what was once the market square. As a town which stood on the main coaching routes, there are many examples of coaching inns, the most obvious being the White Hart, opposite what was the town pump. The yards to the rear of the inns, such as the Kings Arms Yard, are surrounded by buildings of historic interest which now serve as antique shops etc.

St Andrew's church, like all the churches in this area, is built of ironstone. The present building dates back to the fourteenth, fifteenth century with nineteenth- and twentieth-century additions. A memorial of particular interest is one to the north side of the altar commemorating Richard Nicholls (born 1625) and buried here. He was sent as leader of a small military expedition to recover the North American Territories from

The Globe Inn, Linslade, Grand Union Canal
View of Marston Vale

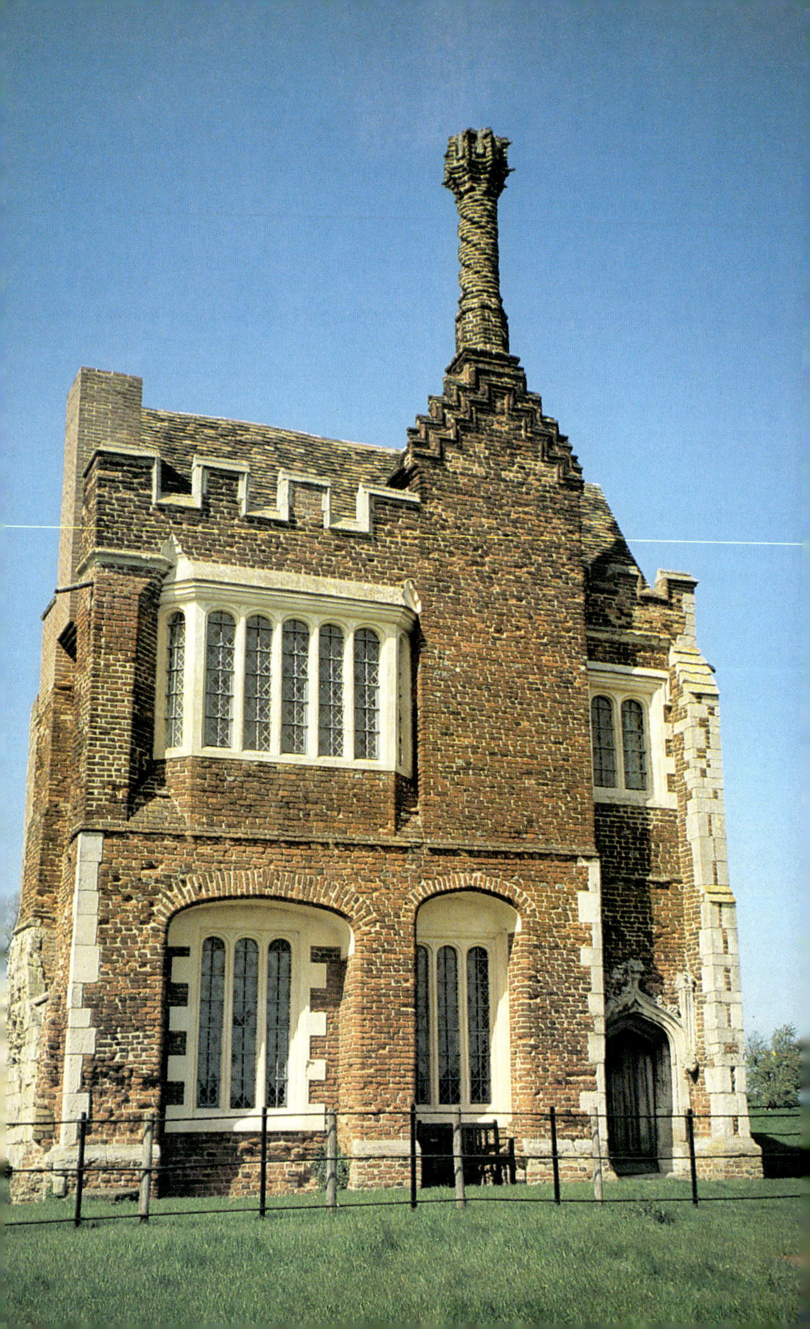

Coaching Inn Yard, Ampthill

Warden Abbey, Old Warden

AN OXBRIDGE WALK

the Dutch. In 1664 he received the surrender of Niew Amsterdam which he renamed New York, after James Duke of York (afterwards James II). The memorial to him not only records his achievements, but also incorporates the Dutch cannonball that killed him in the Battle of Sole Bay (Southwold) in 1672!

In front of the church, the lych gate and almshouses, some of which date back to 1485, complete the picturesque setting of this interesting church.

On the western outskirts of Ampthill is Cooper's Hill Nature Reserve, known locally as "The Firs". It is the best remaining example in Bedfordshire of the heathland which once stretched across the county on the thin acidic soils of the Lower Greensand ridge. On the edge of the site, where Ampthill clay reaches the surface, springs occur which support rich marsh plant communities. The heathland flora is dominated by heather and fine grasses and, together with two woodland areas, a range of habitat exists which supports a diversity of flora and fauna including species of very limited distribution in the county. The site is an SSSI, a large part of which is also a Local Nature Reserve, managed by the Beds and Hunts Naturalists' Trust.

GENERAL INFORMATION

En Route

Of particular interest	Woburn Abbey and Deer Park
	Vehicle proving ground - views
Accommodation	None
Camping	South View Farm, Lidlington (01525) 403777
	Millbrook - The Chequers (01525) 403835
Refreshments	Eversholt - The Green Man
	Millbrook - The Chequers
PO/shops	None
Public phone	Eversholt, Millbrook
Banks	None - nearest, Ampthill
Parking	Eversholt - roadside only
	Millbrook - small car park just outside on GRW
Misc	Eversholt - heated open-air swimming pool (pm summer months only)

Ampthill

Of particular interest	Katherine's Cross, Ampthill Park - views
	Georgian houses, coaching inns
Accommodation	Prince of Wales (01525) 403350
	White Hart (01525) 402158

	Guesthouses:
	One-O-Five (01525) 403778
	Dingley Dells (01525) 840306
	(1m south on Flitwick Rd)
Refreshments	Six pubs, restaurants, cafes
PO/shops	Post office, supermarkets, chemist, gift shops
Public phone	Yes
Banks	Yes
Parking	Free car parks
Tourist information	Council Offices, 12 Dunstable Street (01525) 402051
Misc	Market day - Thurs
Access	Road A507 linking M1(Junct.13) with A6 and A1
	Rail Nearest station - Flitwick or Bedford
	(Thameslink line) (01234) 269686 or
	(Bletchley to Bedford Branch line)
	Lidlington or Millbrook Station (01908) 370883
	Bus (01234) 228337

AMPTHILL - MAULDEN - CLOPHILL - (7 miles)

Of particular interest

Houghton House (ruins of); Maulden Church Meadows and Wood (SSSI); Clophill - ruins of abandoned church (old St Mary's); Detour - Wrest Park House (2m to south of route).

From where the Greensand Ridge Walk (GRW) meets the road above Ampthill, the route turns left, up to the brow of the hill, where it turns right at a way-marked finger-post along a concrete track. A few hundred yards along the track a small car park is passed on the left and a single row of houses on the right. Just past the last house, the route turns right to continue along another track.

The ruins of Houghton House (English Heritage) seen from here on the northern face of the hill, are well worth a visit. A scheduled ancient monument, the house was built in the Jacobean style for the Countess of Pembroke in 1615. It was partly dismantled and gutted in 1794 by its final owner, the Duke of Bedford. Nothing was recorded and little preserved at the time of its destruction and even the mile long avenue of over a thousand trees was cut down that autumn. However, in spite of the Duke of Bedford's

Ampthill to Clophill
7 miles

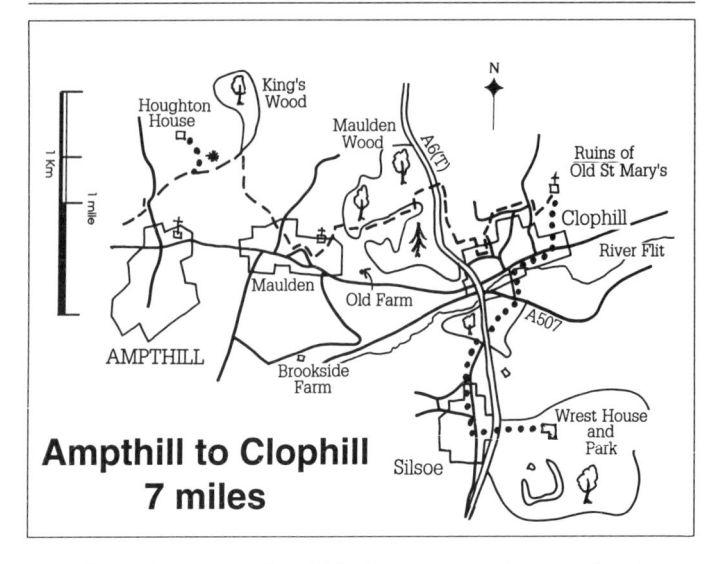

best efforts, the house outlasted him in more ways than one since it was immortalised by Bunyan as "House Beautiful" in his book Pilgrim's Progress.

Records show that Bunyan, Bedfordshire born and bred, visited Houghton House when plying his early trade as a travelling tinker. Later, as the result of a religious awakening, he became a preacher and he wrote his famous book whilst languishing in Bedford gaol, where he was incarcerated for almost 12 years for the "crime" of non-conformist preaching.

Having turned right at the end of the row of houses, the route follows the track along the top of the escarpment with fine views to the north and east across Marston Vale, Bunyan's "Slough of Despond".

This landscape, famous for the landmarks provided by its surviving brickworks chimneys, is due for a face-lift under an ambitious scheme to create 61 square miles of Community Forest over the next 30 years.

The path runs past a white farmhouse on the left, then over a stile and across a pasture to another stile at the corner of King's Wood.

An SSSI and locally managed Nature Reserve accessible to walkers,

LEIGHTON BUZZARD TO GAMLINGAY

Ruins of Houghton House, Ampthill

View of Marston Vale

where bluebells, yellow archangel, wood spurge and other species to be found in ancient woodland flower under the trees.

Over the stile, the route turns at right-angles to head south, across a wide arable field, aiming for a medium sized ash tree where a stile is set in the hedge. After this stile, the route follows a headland path, keeping to the left of the hedge at the bottom corner of the field. Where the hedge ends, a stile leads to a wide track to King's Farm. Just before the farmyard is reached, a finger-post on the left points across the track to the right, where the GRW leaves via another stile. From here the path runs diagonally to the left between the buildings of King's Farm, on the left, and the houses on the outskirts of the village of Maulden, to the right. The route then goes straight over a road and continues along a way-marked path down the left-hand side of a house. Further on, this path merges with a metalled path and continues ahead between more houses to where it meets, and turns left on, a road into the village of Maulden.

Maulden, like many other villages within the Bedford/Luton/Milton Keynes triangle, survives as a dormitory area for commuters. However, some interesting, older buildings intersperse the "housing estate" style bungalows and modern houses. A few hundred yards down the road on the right, for instance, an otherwise unprepossessing red-brick Victorian "semi" proudly displays a large, red tiled plaque complete with a representation of Queen Victoria, "60 years Queen of G. Britain and Ireland, Empress of India". Boldly it proclaims the year in which the house was built (1897), and with supreme confidence in the immutability of the future, lists the "children" of the Queen's Empire: Canada, Australia, New Zealand, Burma, Egypt, Cyprus, Malta, Gibraltar, Africa, West Indies. Those walkers "not amused" will no doubt proceed on their way with dark thoughts about the fate of Ozymandius (Shelley's poem of the same name).

After passing the house described above, the road bears right and about 200 yards further on, the GRW turns left where a waymarked finger-post indicates a metalled path leading up the hill to the village church.

At this point, before going up the path, those looking for refreshments, shops or B+B should continue ahead and down into the main part of the village.

St Mary's Parish Church was largely rebuilt in 1859, but the base of the tower dates from the fifteenth century. The churchyard contains the family mausoleum of the Bruces of Houghton House, the remains of a medieval cross, and trees not typically found in a churchyard, including Corsican pine, lime and giant redwoods. In front of the church is a conveniently sited wooden seat from which to enjoy the wide views to the south.

The route continues from the rear of the churchyard and crosses the car park to the left into Maulden Church Meadow, an ancient pasture designated by the Nature Conservancy Council as an SSSI.

Bedfordshire County Council owns and manages 8½ acres of ancient meadowland as a Local Nature Reserve. This area supports a wide range of wild flowers and grasses which vary according to the two types of subsoil (boulder clay and outcrops of Greensand) found here. Herbs and several species uncommon within the county, including meadow saxifrage and adder's-tongue, have been recorded on the neutral grassland of the boulder clay. The small areas of acidic grassland on the Greensand outcrops are characterised by harebell, sheep's sorrel, common cat's-ear and mouse-ear hawkweed. Apart from the flower rich meadow, the grassland provides an important habitat for butterflies, whilst the three ponds, one of which is permanent, provide breeding grounds for various insects, including dragonflies.

The path traverses the length of the meadow before leaving via the right-hand of two stiles at the far end. From here the path runs through a copse to where a wooden fence marks the boundary of Maulden Wood, another SSSI accessible to walkers.

This is probably the best example of a Greensand wood along the route and is particularly varied since it is partly on a wet clay plateau and partly on sandy soil which is very well drained and leached of nutrients. There are Scots and Corsican pine, European larch, Norway spruce, Lawson's cypress, beech, pedunculate oak and, on the sandy slopes, sweet chestnut. Plant life is similarly varied with pendulous sedge, soft rush, meadowsweet and marsh thistle characteristic of the clay soil to the north, and bluebell and dog's mercury more abundant on the sandy soils to the south. The wood also supports a wide range of breeding birds and 42 species have been counted in the edge of Oak-Ash Woodland bordering pasture, whilst 36 were recorded at a pond in the middle of a Scots Pine Plantation. The species list of plants and insects is exceptional whilst small and large mammals abound, including Muntjac deer, now common throughout Bedfordshire and its neighbouring counties.

Past the fence the route forks to the right and eventually turns left to follow the right-hand edge of the woods. Here, where the boulder clay and the Greensand meet, there is a very clear division between the mainly broad-leaved woods on boulder clay, and the gorse and fir tree covered land to the right. The path undulates over mini hills and valleys, staying on the edge of the wood across the track leading to the thatched Round House until, just before it reaches the house ahead on the right, it turns into the woods. Just inside the woods, the route turns right to follow a path over a footbridge and then straight ahead over a track. From here the path continues in the same direction (ignoring other paths/tracks coming in on both sides), down into and out of a narrow valley, on the other side of which it meets and turns left on a concrete track. The route continues ahead over cross-tracks to eventually meet the main A6(T).

After crossing to the other side of the dual carriage-way, the route turns right along the grass verge which it follows downhill until a stone wall is reached on the left with the remains of a metalled path at its base. At the end of the wall, the GRW turns left at a way-marked finger-post, up the steps in the steep embankment. At the top of the embankment it turns right to follow a headland path around the perimeter of the next two fields. In the second field, the path meets and turns left along a wooden fence at the edge of a disused quarry. The path stays with the fence where it descends a steep bank, at the bottom of which the route turns right along a wide track. The track runs down the side of the quarry, where widespread tree planting is doing something to restore the environment, and eventually meets a road. Here the route turns left into the outskirts of the village of Clophill.

Clophill is another sprawling village which seems to have evolved around two distinct centres. The Stone Jug pub, passed on the left after a few hundred yards, is a good example of the use of the local Greensand stone - it also serves an excellent local "real ale" brewed in the village of Shefford, a few miles to the south.

Just past the pub, the GRW turns left up a cul-de-sac, The Slade, along which B+B is available at number 14, 'House Beautiful'. The lane ends at a sandy track where the route follows a path to the right, up to and through a small-holding stocked in part with a very friendly bunch of free-range Oxford Sandy and Blacks - a rare breed of pigs.

From the small-holding the path carries on ahead to negotiate three more stiles before turning right along a track leading past Kiln Farm. The track becomes Old Kiln Lane leading to a Y junction where the route turns left and then, after a few hundred yards, right at a T junction. After a short distance, the GRW turns left off the road, at a way-marked finger-post along a grassy track leading uphill to the ruins of the abandoned church of St Mary's.

Old St Mary's church was abandoned at the time of the Black Death when surviving villagers retreated to the valley below. The ruins of this church have witnessed scenes of desecration in the more recent past. In March 1963, an eighteenth-century tomb was forced open and the contents removed to be used in black magic ceremonies performed within the ruins of the church. All the gravestones have now been removed and stacked around the churchyard walls.

Abandoned church, Old St Mary's, Clophill

Recommended visit - Wrest Park House and Gardens

At weekends, this point on the route also provides an opportunity to visit Wrest Park House and Gardens - 2 miles each way - same route out and back.

From the abandoned church, the route follows the track leading downhill to the road. Here it turns right and follows the road past the post office before turning left down The Causeway, the lane with the old mill on the corner. When this lane meets the main road, the route crosses to the left to a partially concealed stile on the opposite side of the road on the edge of the woods. From here it continues ahead along a track running through the attractive, mature woodland of Warren Wood. On the other side of the wood, the route meets the busy dual carriageway of the A6 where it turns left along the verge for about 50 yards. It then turns right, across the dual carriage-way, to pick up the roadside footpath on the road opposite leading for about a mile into the village of Silsoe. In the centre of the village, just past the post office, the route turns left up to and through the ornamental iron gates which give access to the main drive leading to Wrest Park House.

Wrest Park House (English Heritage) was built in the nineteenth century, on the site of an earlier house, by Lord De Grey. Like Waddesdon Manor, this very large building was inspired by the eighteenth-century French chateaux. Originally the home of the Dukes of Kent, today it serves mainly as offices, but several rooms, including the grand staircase, can be visited by the public at weekends. The 150 acres of imposing, formal gardens include the semi-formal Great Garden, with a half-mile vista down Long Water flanked by woods. The grandiose style of such buildings as the baroque Pavilion reflect the French influence which at the time extended even to the orange trees in the orangery, which were brought over specially from Versailles. However, the French influence was not allowed to extend to the French statues made of lead which had stood in the grounds of the original house. They were considered to be insufficiently clothed and were sold as scrap! Within the grounds, a number of special events take place

Wrest Park House,
Special Events Day 1993

AN OXBRIDGE WALK

during the summer months, such as falconry displays, a craft festival, and one very special weekend when visitors can see the "eighteenth century brought to life". Members of English Heritage's special events unit don period costume to re-enact scenes in which the "gentry of the 1770s" indulge in "leisure, music and dance". At a discreet distance, at the far end of the grounds, "British Guardsmen" demonstrate the use of cannon and muskets in order to raise volunteers for the war against the American colonists.

For further details (admission charges etc.) tel (01525) 860152.

A Leisure Link bus service to Wrest Park operates May-Sept, Sun or Bank Hol Mon only. (01525) 712132.

GENERAL INFORMATION

En Route

Of particular interest	Houghton House (ruins of)
	Maulden Church Meadows and Wood (SSSI)
Accommodation	Maulden - Hildern Guesthouse (01525) 404630
	Maulden - (1 mile S) - Brookside Farm (01525) 405506
Camping	Maulden - (1 mile E) Old Farm (phone to confirm) (01525) 402162
Refreshments	Maulden - three pubs
PO/shops	Maulden - PO/stores, mini-market
Public phone	Maulden
Banks	None - nearest, Ampthill
Parking	Houghton House - small car park
	Maulden church - car park

Clophill

Of particular interest	Main route -	Ruins of abandoned church (old St Mary's)
	Detour -	visit Wrest Park House (2 miles S - see directions)
Accommodation	House Beautiful (01525) 860517	
Refreshments	Four pubs	
PO/shop	Yes	
Public phone	Yes	
Banks	None - nearest, Ampthill	
Parking	Roadside only	
	St Mary's old church - small parking area	
Access	Road A507 linking M1 (junction 13) with A6(T) and A1(T)	
	Rail No nearby station - access as Ampthill	
	Bus (01234) 228337	

CLOPHILL - HAYNES - (Detour, OLD WARDEN, ICKWELL GREEN) - NORTHILL - (8 miles)

Of particular interest

Main route - View (N) of Cardington sheds, Northill church and pub.

Detour - Old Warden church, thatched cottages, Swiss garden; Shuttleworth Collection of airworthy vintage aircraft, Ickwell Green and Maypole.

The Greensand Ridge Walk (GRW) turns left on the track in front of the ruined church and continues in a northerly direction, keeping to the left of an open gateway, just before which is the first good view of the circular array of aerials of the listening post at RAF Chicksands. Over a stile, the path turns right along the hedge-line on the top of the ridge with views over the valley to the south-west. After a short distance the path turns left with the hedge down the hill and across a footbridge over a narrow stream. Here the route turns right to follow a headland track on the edge of Chicksands Wood, managed by the Forestry Commission.

The headland path follows the edge of the wood for over a mile, eventually running downhill to the road where the route turns left. After about a quarter of a mile, the GRW turns right on a way-marked track up and over an open hillside and through the farmyard of Hill Farm where it meets another road a hundred yards or so to the left of the Greyhound pub.

The GRW turns left along the road for a few hundred yards before turning off right on a way-marked track bearing east across open fields leading to the road at Deadman's Cross.

At the road, The Red Lion pub offers B+B accommodation and is just down the road to the right.

Note a complication at this point on the GRW: In accordance with the terms of the access agreement between the owners and Bedfordshire County Council, the route through Warden Great Wood and Warden Little Wood is closed to walkers during the shooting season - ie. from 1st Nov to 1st Mar.

Clophill to Northill
8 miles

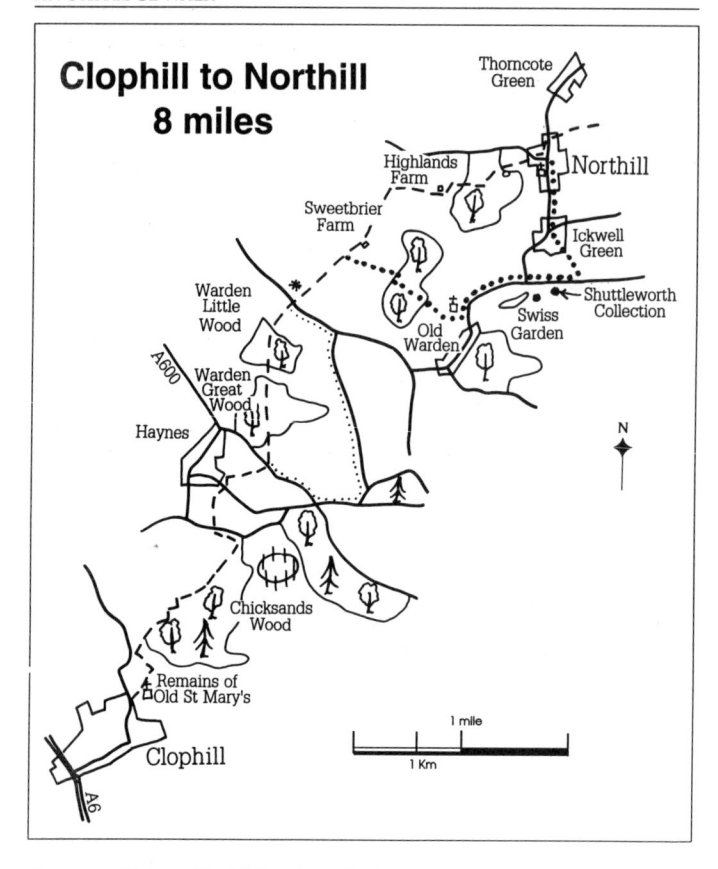

(Map showing route from Clophill to Northill, passing Remains of Old St Mary's, Chicksands Wood, Warden Great Wood, Warden Little Wood, Haynes, Sweetbrier Farm, Highlands Farm, Old Warden, Swiss Garden, Shuttleworth Collection, Ickwell Green, Thorncote Green, and Northill. Scale: 1 mile / 1 Km.)

Summer Route (2nd Mar-31st Oct)

During the summer months, the route crosses over the road and continues in the same direction keeping to the right of a hedge. Where the hedge ends a stile gives access to a path and then a well-surfaced track running through the mixed woodland of Warden Great Wood and Warden Little Wood. The two woods are separated by an arable field and a cross-country horse trials course. On the other side of Warden Little Wood, the track leaves next to the lodge and carries on across an open field to where it meets Bedford Road (the point where the winter route re-joins).

Along the road to the right lies Abbey Farm, Warden Vineyard and a Landmark Trust property available for holiday lets - details shown at end of winter route.

Winter Route (1st Nov-1st Mar)

During this period an extra 2 miles must be walked along roads which avoid the woods. The route turns right along the road past the pub and left at the crossroads. It then keeps going left where the road forks and again further on where it heads across open fields before crossing a bridge over a dismantled railway line just before joining Bedford Road.

After crossing the railway bridge, on the right, is Abbey Farm, built close to the site of the Cistercian Abbey of Warden, founded in 1135 by Walter Espec, who founded Rievaulx Abbey in Yorkshire three years earlier. The land surrounding the site of the Abbey is Greensand over boulder clay and the monks cleared the woodland and planted the original Great Vineyard of 10 acres and the Vineyard field of over 4 acres. After a gap of four centuries, the vineyard at Warden has been replanted and has the distinction of currently being the only vineyard in production in the county of Bedfordshire. The white wines it produces are of high quality and have won awards for the last three consecutive years. (Bottles may be purchased locally at Maggies Farm Shop, Summerfields Fruit Farm, Haynes.) Tours of the vineyard can be arranged, but are by appointment only on the basis of a minimum group of ten. (01462) 811266.

Nothing remains above ground of the Abbey buildings except for a surviving fragment incorporated in what remains of the house built by the Gostwick family. This intriguing remnant is leased to the Landmark Trust, through whom it is available for holiday lets. (01628) 825925.

The winter route turns left along Bedford Road to rejoin the summer route where the GRW is signposted off on a track to the right.

The summer route crosses straight over the road after Warden Little Wood. From here a track runs ahead and after a hundred yards or so crosses over the top of a tunnel on the dismantled old Midland Railway line.

Opened in 1857 this was once the Bedford to Hitchin line, part of the main line to London. *The length of the top of the 882 yards long tunnel has been adopted as a wildlife and nature reserve for the Wildlife Trust and is managed by Bedfordshire and Cambridge County Councils. The tangled growth of hawthorn and bramble scrub provides excellent cover for birds in this arable landscape, whilst the cutting supports a wide variety of grasses and plants protected from agricultural fertilizers and sprays.*

Cardington Airship Sheds loom over the landscape to the north-west as two huge, alien shapes. Over 700ft long, nearly 180ft high and over 270ft in overall width, they were the biggest buildings in the world at the time they were constructed and are the only survivors of their kind in Europe. Cardington is forever associated with the fate of the R101, the huge airship which crashed in Beauvais, in October 1930, on her inaugral flight to India. There were only a few survivors and the remains of the 48 that were killed in the crash and ensuing holocaust are buried in a mass grave in the churchyard of Cardington's Parish Church. Buried with the victims of the crash was also the dream that rigid airships would one day encircle the world from Cardington, optimistically described at the time as "the world's greatest airport".

The track continues straight ahead keeping to the left of the hedge at first and then switching to the other side along a headland path. After some distance, at two way-marked oak-posts in the gap at the end of the first hedgerow across the line of march, there is a chance to include a detour to the main route which only adds about a mile to the overall distance. Those who wish to continue along the GRW at this point should refer to the section headed "Main Route", below.

Detour route

OLD WARDEN VILLAGE & CHURCH - THE SWISS GARDEN - SHUTTLEWORTH COLLECTION - ICKWELL VILLAGE & GREEN
This detour is strongly recommended as it has a high concentration of places of particular interest with B+B available at the PO/shop in Old Warden village.

From the headland path, the route turns right, following the hedge and the blue circular walk signs. At the corner of the first field, it crosses a footbridge and continues in the same direction keeping to the right of the hedge. In the corner of the field the path turns right for about 50 yards along the edge of Palmers Wood, before turning left into the wood following a broad track.

Palmers Wood contains areas of ancient woodland including stands of hornbeam, an unusual tree in Bedfordshire, and other uncommon, native trees. The wood is a haven for a variety of birdlife and in the spring this wood, and the surrounding woodlands, are awash with the heavily scented haze of bluebells.

On the other side of the woods, the route carries over a cross tracks and across a field to follow the edge of a small wood on the left. At the end of the wood, the path leads through a wooden gate and across a rough pasture, heading for the tower of Old Warden church in front of which a small car park provides sturdy wooden benches in a delightful setting.

St Leonard's church is of twelfth-century origins and its exterior, in the words of Pevsner, does nothing "to prepare for the shock in store upon entering". In 1841, the interior was extensively altered for Lord Ongley and fitted out with a miscellany of carved woodwork from the Continent. A riot of two-headed snakes and fabulous beasts are carved into the box pews, the pulpit, the font-cover and panelled walls. A raised wooden gallery runs to the right of the entrance door and great carved oak beams support the roof. The Ongley family, which originally owned and created the Old Warden estates, lies buried within the vaults of the mausoleum in the churchyard not far from the family grave of the Shuttleworths, who subsequently owned these estates. The church porch contains a poignant inscription in memory of Richard Ormonde Shuttleworth, Pilot Officer, RAFVR, the "last squire of Old Warden", who "gave his life, 2nd August, 1940".

Old Warden village has a pub and some of the prettiest thatched cottages along the entire route. However, those walkers who want to carry on to the Shuttleworth Collection without visiting the village first, should turn left down the lane leading to the church and left again where the lane meets the road.

Those visiting the village, or in need of B+B, should take the path through the iron swing gates immediately opposite the church. (To the left can be seen what is now the Shuttleworth Agricultural College set in parkland next to a lake.) The route to the village continues through another swing-gate in the corner of the first field and then follows the hedge to where a steep flight of steps on the left descends into a third field.

From here the path keeps to the right of the hedge and fence to the road in the centre of the village where the route turns left.

Here the Hare and Hounds pub has a restaurant offering a menu throughout the day. Next door is the village shop and post office which is also a tea gardens at weekends during the summer and has B+B accommodation.

Having turned left along the road past the pub, the route stays with the road for a good half a mile before keeping to the right where the road forks. Eventually, on the right, the entrance to the Swiss Garden is reached to the rear of a small aircraft hangar.

The Swiss Garden was once part of the grounds and gardens of the nearby house, now Shuttleworth Agricultural College. It is a 10 acre, romantic, fantasy garden, with pathways that wind round tiny ponds and over intricate, ironwork bridges. Amongst the decorative structures to be found in the garden is a tiny Swiss cottage, a miniature "chapel", a brilliantly coloured Indian kiosk, and a fernery and grotto. The overall effect is a bit "Alice in Wonderland", especially the grotto which only needs Alice's white rabbit rushing past muttering "I'm late, I'm late" to complete its fairytale atmosphere.

For serious gardeners the gardens also contain some magnificent tree specimens, early types of rambling rose, and a superb collection of ferns. The garden is particularly colourful in spring, when great banks of azaleas and rhododendrons are in bloom.

The garden is open Apr-Oct, every afternoon, (closed Tues). Sun, from 10am. During the winter the garden is closed Nov and Dec. Jan-Mar it opens Sun only, from 11am. A free lakeside picnic area is also accessible.

For further details (admission charges etc.) tel (01234) 228330.

After the Swiss Garden, the

Swiss Garden, Old Warden

route continues along the road, past the aircraft hangar, to the gates of the Shuttleworth Collection.

The Shuttleworth Collection is based at Old Warden aerodrome, an old-fashioned airfield consisting of seven hangars and a grass landing field. Five hangars contain a range of nearly 40 aircraft, ranging from the 1909 Bleriot, to famous aircraft of both World Wars and examples of de Havillands from the interwar years. What makes this collection so special is that nearly all the aircraft on permanent display are airworthy and take part in the programme of flying displays organised throughout the summer months. These occasions are famous for providing a chance to see aircraft in the air that are rarely, if ever, seen elsewhere. On display days, the Shuttleworth Collection at Old Warden becomes something very special,

*DH 51 - the only airworthy specimen of de Havilland's oldest design
(by kind permission of The Shuttleworth Collection)*

much more than just a living museum.

The static exhibition, shop, restaurant and car park are open throughout the year, except over Christmas and up to and including New Year's Day.

Admission times are 10am-4pm, 3pm Nov-Mar. Flying displays, including Sundown Flying Displays, are usually held at weekends.

For further details (admission charges etc.) tel (01767) 627288.

Several hundred yards along the road past the main entrance to the Shuttleworth Collection, the route turns left along a bridleway which keeps to the left of a hedge and ditch across an arable field before running ahead between fences to emerge at the bottom of Ickwell Green.

Ickwell Green is famous throughout the county for its permanent Maypole and May Day celebrations have been taking place on the green since at least 1563. Such celebrations were important in rural communities and would not only have included the traditional dance round the Maypole by the children, but also pageants with fiddling and dancing. There would have been a "dragon" and a hobby horse, and Morris dancers with bells fastened to elbows, knees and ankles. In addition to the Maypole, a huge oak dominates the cricket pitch on the village green which is also overlooked by colour washed, thatched cottages. Thomas Tompion, the "father of English clock-making", lived in one of the nearby cottages. He was born and grew up in this parish, became a leading watchmaker at the court of Charles II, was honoured in his lifetime, and buried at Westminster Abbey in 1713.

From the bottom of the green a small service road runs ahead past the cottages and village school on the right before crossing over Caldecote Road. From here it continues along a metalled path up to the road where it turns right on a roadside path. The route stays with the road for a good half-mile to the T junction next to the church in the village of Northill, where the detour route rejoins the GRW.

Just before the T junction is The Crown Inn. This inn has a colourful history and is reputed to be haunted by a ghostly monk, who has been wandering its corridors for centuries. Underground passages once linked the inn with the nearby grange and the church, but these have now been blocked by falls of earth.

Main Route

The GRW continues straight ahead and then turns right before going through a hedge on the other side of which it meets a sandy track just above Sweetbrier farmhouse. Here the route turns left on a sandy track which follows the straggling edge of a narrow belt of woodland, keeping ahead over the first cross-tracks to turn right on a way-marked track at the next junction. From here the track runs past the left-hand end of a solitary hedge-line and down to the bottom of the hill where it dog-legs left, then right, through a belt of trees. On the other side of the tree belt a stile and path leads across a narrow pasture and up the rise keeping to the right of Highlands Farm. Over another stile, the path heads diagonally left across a pasture in front of the farmhouse to almost the bottom corner where a second stile takes it through another belt of trees. On the other side of the trees, it turns right as a headland path running round a large arable field with mixed woodland on the right. After travelling a good distance round the field, the route turns right on a way-marked track into the woods. In the middle of the woods, it turns left along a broad track for a few hundred yards, before turning right, keeping ahead over two cross-tracks after which it emerges at the bottom of rising land currently cultivated as a market garden.

On the right are a series of small ponds, thought to be the remnants of a complex of medieval fish ponds, whilst just clearing the rise in front can be seen the top of the square tower of Northill church.

The route follows the track up and over the rise after which it meets and turns right on the road into the village of Northill. At the T junction next to the church the GRW turns left, at which point the main route is also rejoined by the detour route.

St Mary's church contains a list of incumbents dating back to 1224. A room above the porch was originally a chapel and subsequently served as a school room until 1850. The interior of the church is particulary impressive, with two stained glass windows commissioned by the Grocer's Company, patrons of the church. There is a great oak chest dated 1663 in which the parish records were kept and a seventeenth-century Tompion bier bearing the legend "After death cometh judgement". A very comprehensive and informative guide to the church and the immediate district is on sale in the church.

Just the other side of the church, down the road to the right, is The Crown pub.

LEIGHTON BUZZARD TO GAMLINGAY

GENERAL INFORMATION

En Route

Of particular interest	Main route -	View of Cardington sheds
	Detour -	Old Warden church, thatched cottages
		Swiss garden
		Shuttleworth Collection of vintage aircraft
		Ickwell Green and Maypole
Accommodation		Haynes' Deadman's Cross - The Red Lion (01234) 381381
		Old Warden, post office & guest house (01767) 627201
		Westcott, Upper Caldecote (1m E on road from aerodrome) - (01767) 315882
Camping		Haynes - Summerfields, Rook Tree Farm (under 1m NW on A600) (01234) 381400
Refreshments		Haynes - one pub
		Deadman's Cross - one pub
		Old Warden - one pub, tea gardens, cafe (Shuttleworth Collection)
PO/shops		Haynes - PO/store
		Old Warden - PO/store
Public phone		Deadman's Cross, Haynes, Old Warden
		Shuttleworth Collection, Ickwell Green
Banks		None - nearest, Sandy
Parking		Old Warden - St Leonard's Church, small car park
		Swiss garden car park
		Shuttleworth Collection car park

Northill

Of particular interest		Church and pub
Accommodation		Village Farm, Thorncote Green (01767) 627345 (half a mile north of T junction)
Camping		Village Farm (as above)
Refreshments		One pub
PO/shop		No
Public phone		No (nearest, Ickwell Green or Thorncote Green)
Bank		No, nearest Sandy
Parking		Roadside only
Access		Road S of Sandy off A1(T)
	Rail	Nearest station, Sandy
		(London to Peterborough Line) (01234) 269686
	Bus	(01234) 228337

AN OXBRIDGE WALK

NORTHILL - SANDY - EVERTON - GAMLINGAY - (9 miles)

Of particular interest

Sandy, RSPB HQ (Reserve and Visitors' Centre); Ex-RAF Tempsford (SOE); Gamlingay - church and nearby houses.

At the T junction, the Greensand Ridge Walk (GRW) turns left on Thorncote Road. After passing Copelands Farm on the left-hand side of the road, the route leaves the road via a way-marked track on the right.

Stay on the road for another half mile for B+B or camping at Village Farm, Thorncote Green.

Having left the road, the track heads off across open fields with the mast of Sandy TV transmitter ahead to the north-east. After crossing a footbridge over a wide drainage ditch it dog-legs left,

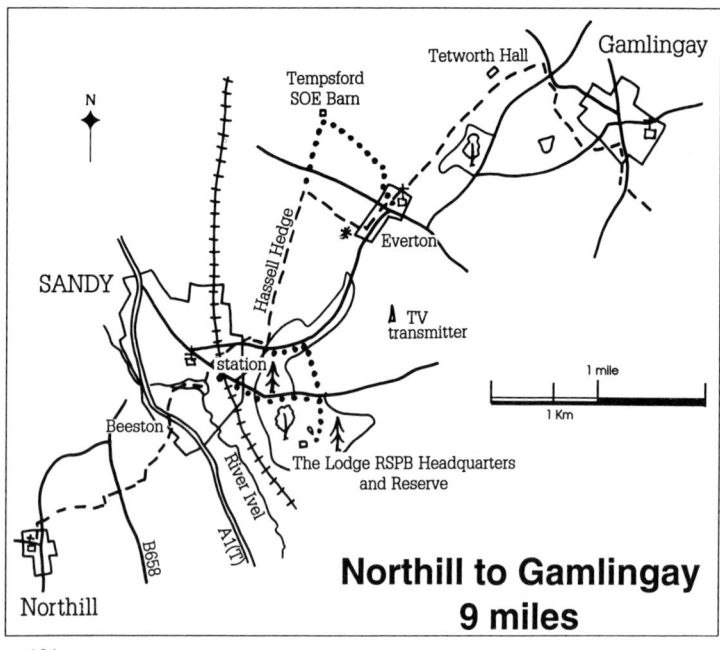

Northill to Gamlingay
9 miles

Greensand Ridge Walk, nr Northill

then right, over flat fields until it meets the road which it crosses straight over.

This stretch of the route, as far as Sandy, crosses the flat, intensely cultivated plain of the Ivel Valley. Market gardening on a grand scale, with acres of crops under glass cloches, makes this an interesting contrast to the rest of the route through Bedfordshire. In fact, a distant line of Lombardy Poplars on the left and the almost total absence of hedges gives the landscape an almost foreign feel.

The path continues ahead in the same general direction, twice turning left and right and heading for a large, white farmhouse (Elm Farm) on the outskirts of Beeston. The route goes straight over the green in front of the farmhouse and turns left along the road. After a few hundred yards the GRW turns right into a cul-de-sac, The

Crescent, at the end of which a footpath leads to a large footbridge spanning the main A1(T) road to the north.

This is the old Great North Road, once the main route to the north out of London and still heavily used in spite of the network of motorways constructed in the postwar years. Just how busy this road is is made only too apparent to walkers, since for a short distance the GRW turns left along the roadside footpath in the face of the on-coming traffic!

A clearly visible and heavily used shortcut across the field from the footbridge is not a public right-of-way.

After about a hundred yards or so along the roadside path, the GRW turns right up a back lane called The Baulk. At the end of this road a metalled path leads to a small bridge over a mill-stream which once served a nearby mill demolished in the 1970s. From here the path continues to a bridge over the River Ivel next to a weir. At this point the river has divided into two arms and the route turns right to follow one arm of the river up to and across another bridge to enter the back streets on the outskirts of the market town of Sandy. After the bridge the route follows the road ahead bearing right to where it meets the main road.

Here, those wishing to continue along the GRW cross straight over. The RSPB HQ detour turns right along the main road, the market town of Sandy is to the left.

Sandy was once an important Roman centre as evidenced by local archaeological finds. Today, it is a busy market town and a useful staging post on the Oxbridge route since it is the last town of any size between here and Cambridge. Communications are good in that it lies on a major trunk-road and also has a main-line railway station. In addition, it has good facilites for travellers including B+B accommodation, car parks, a wide range of restaurants and several banks. It also marks the stage at which a choice of route is available which does not add any overall mileage, but which does offer "twitchers", or walkers with an interest in bird-watching, an opportunity to visit The Lodge, a nature reserve and Headquarters of the RSPB.

Recommended detour - The Lodge, RSPB HQ

From where the GRW meets the main road, the detour route turns right, along the B1042. After crossing the railway bridge the road continues ahead and climbs the long hill of Sandy Warren, a major landmark in the east of the county. Almost at top of this hill, on the right, is the entrance to The Lodge, Headquarters of the RSPB. *The Lodge, designed in the Tudor style by Henry Clutton, was built in 1870 for Viscount Peel, youngest son of Sir Robert. It stands in 43 hectares (106 acres) of mixed woodlands and gardens and contains a surviving area of heathland which once stretched from here along the line of the Greensand as far as Woburn. Forty-two acres have been designated an SSSI. The house, which serves as the administrative headquarters of the RSPB, is not open to the public, but the grounds and gardens are. These contain a number of walks and nature trails with a chance to watch birds from observation hides. There is a wildlife garden and picnic area. The largest shop operated by the RSPB offers a wide range of gifts, bird equipment and optics. A car park and WC is available to visitors. For further details (admission charges etc.) tel (01767) 680551).*

On leaving The Lodge, the detour route crosses over the road to pick up the bridle way opposite the entrance to The Lodge. This broad track runs across open fields before forking left at a pine tree plantation. From here it keeps to the edge of the woods before running through a belt of trees on the other side of which it meets and turns left along the road. Eventually, the road runs downhill and the route takes the right-hand fork at the bottom signposted "No entry for vehicles". Just past this sign, the detour route rejoins the GRW which turns right along a way-marked bridle-path.

Main Route

The GRW crosses straight over the main road and up the way-marked road opposite. After about a hundred yards, it turns right along another road for a short distance and then turns left on a metalled footpath past the left-hand end of a line of garages. Past the garages the path leads to a pedestrian bridge over the railway, on the other side of which a path leads ahead across a short field and up to the woodland area known as The Pinnacle. The GRW follows the branded oak posts through the woods to emerge onto a lane where it turns right. The lane runs through mature woodland before descending a small hill at the bottom of which, just before another road is joined, the GRW turns left on a way-marked bridle-path.

This is also the point where the main route is rejoined by the detour route from the RSPB HQ.

From where it turns left along the bridleway, the route follows along the bottom of the Greensand Ridge. Along this stretch of the ridge, the upper slopes are generally used as sheep pastures, whilst the wide, flat fields at its base are arable farmland. The path crosses wide sheep pastures then passes through an open gateway and under a line of pylons to a five-bar gate. From here it turns right along a headland path following the line of an old Roman road and an ancient boundary known as Hassell Hedge. After two long, arable fields, the headland path becomes a concrete track which eventually leads past farm buildings and the farm-road to Waterloo Farm on the left. Just after passing the farm buildings the GRW turns right on a way-marked track.

At this point there is a choice of either staying with the main route or of including a visit to the site of one of the best kept secrets of World War Two.

Highly recommended detour - Site of RAF Tempsford

The detour route carries on ahead then crosses straight over a road to follow a concrete track. This track shortly joins what is left of the old perimeter track round the airfield. To the left, on the far side of what was the airfield, can be seen various buildings, including a surviving hangar.

During World War Two, Tempsford served as a base for special operations carried out by 161 and 138 squadrons of the RAF. One of the best-known COs of 161 Squadron was Percy Charles Pickard, DSO and two bars, DFC, famous to the wartime public as the pilot of F for Freddie in the film Target for Tonight. *The first RAF officer to be awarded two bars to his DSO, after leaving Tempsford, he was killed in action in February 1944, flying a Mosquito of No 487 Squadron, RNZAF, whilst leading the epic raid on the prison at Amiens.*

The perimeter track runs past the end of what is left of one of the remaining runways, just beyond which is an innocuous looking barn - the nearest thing to a wayside shrine on this "pilgrimage" from Oxford to Cambridge.

SOE (Special Operations Executive) agents were despatched into enemy occupied Europe from Tempsford. This barn is where they received final instructions and were kitted out in accordance with the needs of their mission and the means of their delivery - parachutes if going in by Halifaxes, perilous night landings at secret rendezvous if by Lysanders.

Many and legendary were the operations mounted from Tempsford. Over a thousand agents were either dropped, landed and/or collected from here but it is a sobering thought that many of them failed to return and many aircrew were lost. A noticeboard inside the barn, put up by the East Anglian Aviation Society, reads: "Erected to commemorate the brave deeds of the men and women who flew from this war-time airfield to the forces of the resistance in France, Norway, Holland and other countries during the years 1942 - 1945. The equipment for their dangerous missions was issued to them from this barn". Under this board wreaths of poppies have been placed and rows of small wooden crosses commemorate the aircrew that died. Another board is covered with messages and remembrance cards from people all round the world, including a card left by a Dane claiming that no less than three SOE agents once dropped by parachute within a few hundred yards of his house! There are messages left by relatives, by children, and by walkers who have stumbled on this very special place.

A well-kept secret in wartime, Tempsford remains unknown to the majority of the peacetime population and no official marker or monument has been erected in memory of those who gave their lives. As you walk away from this place, therefore, be mindful of the fact that for those who did not return, this was their last sight of England before taking off on their final missions.

From the barn, the detour route follows the circular walk which leads off the perimeter track to the right. This is a substantial track with steep embankments on both sides which bears right up the side of the hill at the top of which lies the village of Everton. After passing some attractive thatched cottages at the top of the hill, the path finally emerges at Church End, opposite the village church.

From here the GRW follows the road to the left. The Thornton Arms pub lies a few hundred yards along to the right.

Main Route

Just past the farm buildings of Waterloo Farm, the GRW turns right along a way-marked track. The concrete track eventually becomes a field path leading ahead, via three stiles, up to the top of the ridge with fine views to the north-west. A track leads from the third stile to the road where the route turns left into the village of Everton. After passing the village post office/shop, the route turns left down Church Road, to the left of the Thornton Arms pub, and after a few hundred yards passes the village church of St Mary's.

St Mary's church looks out of proportion in relation to the height of its tower because the tower was struck by lighting in 1974 and this resulted in a reduction in its height. The churchyard is interesting and among those buried here is John Berridge who accompanied John Wesley on many of his preaching travels. Wesley himself preached in Everton - but not in the church.

The GRW continues over a cattle grid and through gates on a private road which runs along the top of the ridge for about a mile across pasture and parkland surrounding Storey Farm, Woodbury Hall and some fine examples of nineteenth-century estate style cottages. Eventually, the road bears off to the left, but the GRW keeps straight on across the grass to a kissing-gate next to a white field gate. From here the path carries on across a narrow pasture on the other side of which a stile gives access to a track where the route turns right and then almost immediately left at an oak tree. The route now becomes a headland path across arable fields before crossing a tarmacked drive via a gate, and then over an open pasture with Tetworth Hall (c.1710) on the left, just on the Cambridgeshire side of the border.

The GRW crosses the drive to Tetworth Hall and then goes over another small pasture to a gate leading to a broad track past a thatched cottage. It stays with this metalled track until it reaches another cottage on the left-hand side, where the track bears to the right. Here the route carries straight on, following the line of the hedge. After crossing over two more pastures, it meets and turns right along a lane which leads down to a crossroads at Gamlingay Cinques. Here the route continues ahead, down Cinques Road, and, after about a hundred yards, reaches a small car park on the right.

This car park marks the end of the Greensand Ridge Walk, the longest stretch of continuous pathway on the Oxbridge route. It is also where the Clopton Way begins, the first half of the Oxbridge route from here to Cambridge.

From the official noticeboard at the front of the car park, the

Clopton Way follows a path running diagonally left across the front of two cottages. It then turns right between these two cottages and another pair, on a track which leads for about 200 yards past a barn on the left and along to a new house on the same side. Just past this house, the route turns left on a headland track known as Park Lane. Some distance down this track, before reaching the hedge crossing the line of march, the route passes through the hedge on the left to follow a track between hedges, once part of the old road to York.

Eventually, the track meets a road where the route turns left for a few hundred yards and then right down a way-marked lane known as West Road. The route keeps to the left where the lane forks and, after a few hundred yards, arrives at a T junction. Here those continuing along the Clopton Way turn right, those visiting Gamlingay first, turn left.

Gamlingay was a large and prosperous village throughout the Middle Ages. However, in 1600 a disasterous fire destroyed 76 houses, as a result of which the village declined in importance and lost its market. In spite of the fire, no fewer than 58 buildings in the village are listed by the Royal Commission on Historical Monuments, and the High Street contains some interesting and picturesque buildings. One very fine example, "The Emplins", a half-timbered, medieval hall-house, offers B+B accommodation. North of the village is a vineyard where wine may be sampled and bought.

GENERAL INFORMATION

En Route

Of particular interest	Sandy - RSPB HQ (Reserve and Visitors' Centre)
	Detour - Ex RAF Tempsford (SOE)
Accommodation	Sandy - The Pantiles (01767) 680668
	- The Kings Arms (01767) 680276
	- Fair Lawn Hotel (01767) 680368
	- Highfield Farm (1 mile N) (01767) 682332
Refreshments	Sandy - restaurants, cafes, pubs
	Everton - one pub
PO/shop	Sandy - post office, supermarkets
	Everton - village stores
Public phone	Sandy, Everton
Banks	Sandy

Parking	Sandy, large, free car park in High St
	Everton - roadside and limited in front of church
	Gamlingay Cinques - small car park at start of Clopton Way
Tourist Information	Sandy - library (01767) 680384
General	Sandy - market day Fri

Gamlingay

Of particular interest	Church and houses nearby
Accommodation	The Emplins (near church) (01767) 50581
	(No budget accommodation in Gamlingay)
Refreshments	Three pubs
PO/shops	PO, butcher, pharmacy, general stores, small co-op
Public phone	Yes
Bank	Yes
Parking	Roadside only
Access	Road E of A1(T) on B1040
	Rail As Northill
	Bus Beds (01234) 228337 Cambs (01223) 423554

Tetworth Hall, nr Gamlingay
The Clopton Way, approaching site of medieval village of Clopton

King's College Chapel
Cambridge from St Mary's Church Tower

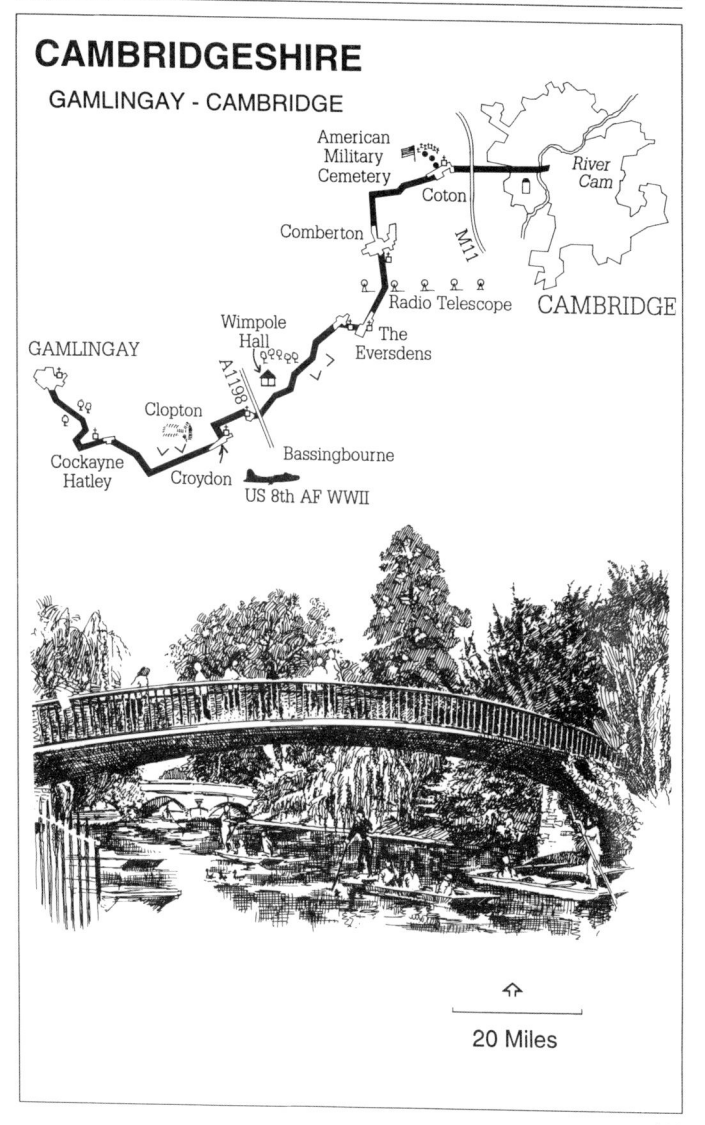

CAMBRIDGESHIRE
GAMLINGAY - CAMBRIDGE

American Military Cemetery
River Cam
Coton
Comberton
M11
Radio Telescope
CAMBRIDGE
Wimpole Hall
The Eversdens
GAMLINGAY
A1198
Clopton
Cockayne Hatley
Croydon
Bassingbourne
US 8th AF WWII

20 Miles

AN OXBRIDGE WALK

Gamlingay to Cambridge: 20 miles

GAMLINGAY - COCKAYNE HATLEY - CROYDON - ARRINGTON - (Wimpole Hall) - (9 miles)

Of particular interest

Cockayne Hatley church and churchyard; Site of medieval village of Clopton; Wimpole Hall and Garden; Wimpole Park, Chinese bridge, Gothic folly, lake; Wimpole Home Farm (rare breeds centre, museum).

This part of the route follows the way-marked Clopton Way. From the end of West Street, in Gamlingay, the route turns right on the roadside path along Mill Street. After clearing the village it continues past a saddlery, then Millbridge Farm and Brookfield Farm to a finger-post on the left, opposite The Two Brewers Cottage, which is where the way-marked Clopton Way leaves the road.

From here the route follows a wide track ahead up Mill Hill towards Potton Wood, crossing a wide sweep of cereal crops stretching to the horizon on either side. At the crest of the hill there are good views behind to the west along the line of march and over the surrounding farmland. The track bears left before turning right between wooden posts and railings as it enters Potton Wood.

The edge of the woods also marks the county boundary and from here to the other side of the village of Cockayne Hatley, the route is back inside the borders of Bedfordshire. The path through Potton Wood, an SSSI, is available by agreement with the Forestry Commission. The woodland is of the wet ash-maple type and the ground flora and rides are rich in species such as bluebell, dog's mercury and wood anemone. The wood also provides a refuge for breeding birds in an otherwise mainly arable landscape.

In the middle of the woods, the route turns left, to follow a grassy track with a line of electricity poles on the right. Keep straight on, ignoring any other paths, until another line of electricity poles comes in from the left, at which point the route turns right along a track leading to a wooden gate. From here the route turns left along

Gamlingay to Arrington (Wimpole Hall)
9 miles

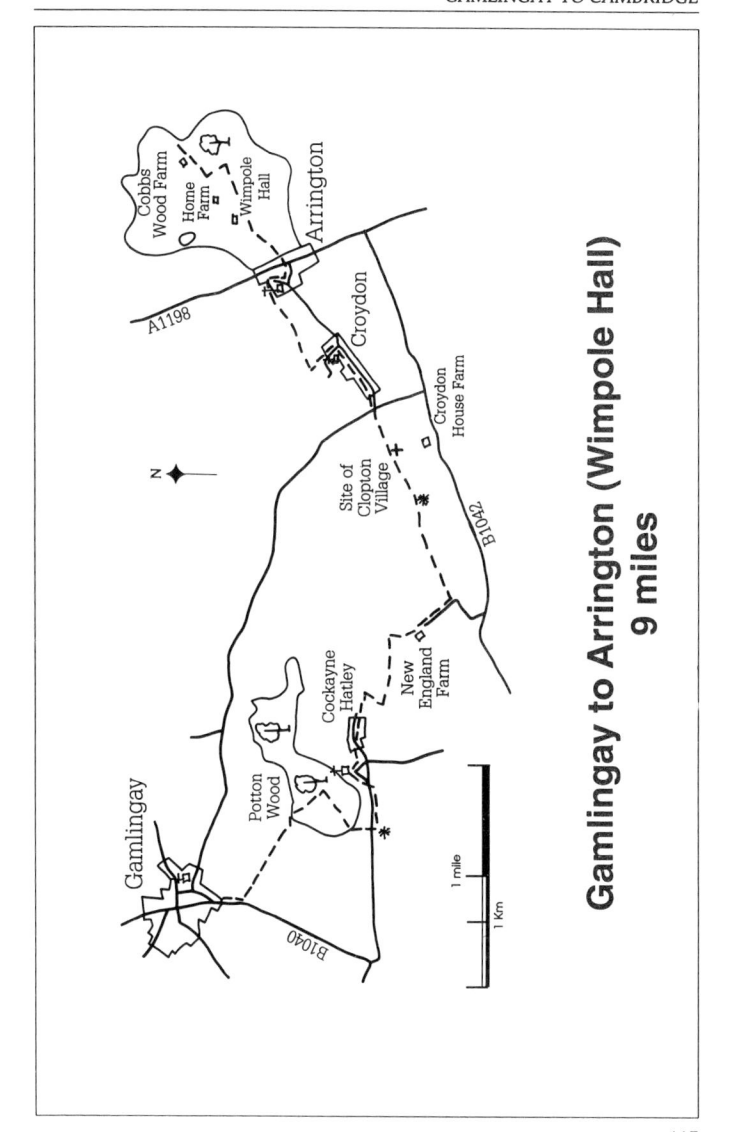

a path leading up to a large water tower where it turns left again along the road.

For the next few miles the advantage of being on even modestly high uplands in a relatively flat landscape becomes obvious as glorious views open up across countryside to the south.

At the second cottage on the left-hand side of the road, the route turns left along the drive leading to the church of St John the Baptist, Cockayne Hatley.

The church of St John the Baptist is built of brown cobbles and was restored in the early 1800s after years of neglect. As a Grade 1 listed building, the church is considered to be of outstanding architectural interest and English Heritage have contributed financial aid towards the cost of its upkeep and repair. The interior of the church is best known for the quality of its baroque woodwork, which comes mainly from Belgium. The churchyard is very pleasant without the walls that make many other churchyards so claustrophobic. W.E.Henley, a nineteenth century poet and man of letters, is buried here. Today, his poetry is largely forgotten, but the man himself has achieved a degree of literary immortality although not, perhaps, of the kind for which he was hoping. Having suffered the amputation of a leg, Henley used a large wooden crutch to get about and his friend, the writer R.L.Stevenson, is thought to have used him as the inspiration for the creation of one of the best known rogues in English fiction, Long John Silver in Treasure Island. *Not to be outdone, his daughter is said to have been the inspiration for Wendy in J.M.Barrie's book* Peter Pan. *Barrie was a frequent visitor to the house and Henley's daughter was in the habit of referring to Barrie as her father's "fwendy".*

Just before the church, the Clopton Way turns right along the road on the perimeter of the unenclosed churchyard. Where the churchyard ends the route turns left on a path along the edge of the churchyard and after a few yards bears right across an arable field. On the other side of the field the route turns left along the road which runs through the hamlet of Cockayne Hatley.

Cockayne Hatley is representative of the way in which changing practices in agriculture have profoundly affected not just the landscape, but also a way of life. Once it stood at the centre of thousands of acres of Cox's Orange apple trees and the area produced huge quantities of what is arguably the best apple in the world. The prewar owner of the estate is fondly remembered by ex-employees for his philanthropy and mild eccentricity. A story is told, for instance, of how he once gave his chauffeur a tip of 25 apple trees! After the Second World War, the Co-op took over the tradition of enlightened ownership and in the apple picking season Co-op workers were bussed up from London on day-trips. They arrived, complete with the crates of stout on board, and returned after a day in the fields sunburnt and loaded down with as many bags of apples as they could carry! Today, prairie-like fields of cereal crops stretch as far as the eye can see and it does not take much imagination to realise that more than the hedges and the apple trees have gone forever. The Co-op still owns the land, but an agricultural industry that once employed and supported an entire community is now said to employ just three men - two workers and a manager!

On the other side of Cockayne Hatley, the Clopton Way continues ahead along a way-marked, easy to follow track across undulating uplands. After a short distance the track bends right, and, about a hundred yards further on, left, down a dip at the bottom of which it passes between two ash trees. At the top of the rise in front, the main track turns right, but the Clopton Way continues ahead

"Prairies", east of Cockayne Hatley

AN OXBRIDGE WALK

following the line of a headland path. After following the line of a newly planted hedge in the first field, the route continues along a mature hedge for several hundred yards in the second field before turning right to follow the line of a ditch. It then turns left at a way-marked oak-post where the path leads across a field and through the farmyard of New England Farm (B+B accommodation available). From in front of the farmhouse the route follows a farm-road with a line of poplars on the left-hand side. It then stays with this road until it turns sharply right, at which point the route turns left on a way-marked track indicated by a finger-post.

After clearing the hedge on the right of this ancient trackway, the full sweep of the countryside to the south is revealed and continues to be so as the route follows the brow of the escarpment for the next 2 miles or so. After crossing a concrete farm road, the route carries on ahead eventually reaching a swing gate followed by a stile, between which a series of mounds and hollows mark the site of the abandoned medieval village of Clopton (after which this middle-distance path is named).

Once a fairly substantial village, with at least 19 households at the time of the Domesday Book, Clopton grew in importance to include a church along with a rectory, two moated manor houses, a mill, a cobbled market-place and a population of around 600. The Black Death decimated the village and the subsequent land enclosures sealed the fate of the survivors. Eventually, the village was abandoned, the parish became extinct and was joined to nearby Croydon. Several fields below the site of Clopton can be seen Croydon House Farm (B+B accommodation available).

After Clopton the path crosses arable fields and eventually meets a road which the route crosses straight over to follow a road which leads through the village of Croydon.

Croydon is a small, pleasant village with a pub at its centre and a church on its outskirts. The village has no less than five deserted medieval moated sites and, by the late seventeenth century, had become part of the estate of the Downing family. Many records and maps relating to the village have been preserved in Downing College, a Cambridge University college endowed by the family and named after them.

The Queen Adelaide allows back-packing customers to over-night in the field behind the pub.

At the end of the High Street, the route turns left, at the War Memorial, to follow the road up past the church.

All Saints was built on an unstable site, as can be seen from the angles of the walls and arcades, and the tower has been recently repaired and strengthened. Sir George Downing, founder of Downing College, is buried in the vaults.

Past the church, at the top of the rise where the road turns sharply left, the route continues straight ahead along a way-marked path to the right of the trees. Where the trees end the path turns right across a narrow field to a way-marked post. From here it continues ahead, keeping to the right of a ditch and, further along, a hedge. The path then crosses a footbridge and turns right along a farm-track. At the light brick barns on the left, the path dog-legs through to the other side of the hedge and runs uphill on a headland path on the edge of a small wood. After a few hundred yards it turns left, over a stile, and then runs diagonally right across an open pasture to where the path meets a lane opposite some newish bungalows. From here the route turns right along Church End, and left at the main road next to the church of St Nicholas. After a short distance along the main road, this section of the Oxbridge route ends at a T junction in the centre of the village of Arrington.

Arrington lines both sides of the main A1198 (Ermine Street, the Roman road which linked London with Lincoln and York). To the right of the T junction is the Georgian Hardwicke Arms Hotel (B+B accommodation available).

About 2 miles south of here, on the main road, is Bassingbourne, a wartime airfield now occupied by the army. During World War Two, the Glenn Miller band came to Bassingbourne to entertain the "Ragged Irregulars", 91st Bomb Group of the American Eighth Air Force. The film Memphis Belle *is a reminder that during the war virtually the whole of East Anglia was one vast airfield from which round the clock operations were mounted by the RAF and the USAAF. Today we walk peaceful countryside that once reverberated to the roar of 1000 bombers overhead. Many of these aircraft and their crews did not return but, flying from Bassingbourne, the* Memphis Belle *beat the odds and was the first B17 "Flying Fortress" bomber in the American Eighth Air Force to complete a tour of duty intact. As the first "ship" to survive 25 successful missions she lifted the fighting morale of an entire air force and on 9th June 1943 she and her crew flew home in triumph.*

B17s can still be seen in the skies over East Anglia today, flying from nearby Duxford, part of the Imperial War Museum, the "Biggest and Best Aeroplane Museum in Europe".

Wimpole Hall is half a mile across the park, through the ornamental gates to the left of the T junction. It is described here, rather than at the start of the next section, since Arrington has B+B accommodation for those who may wish to spend time exploring Wimpole Hall's many attractions before tackling the last stage of the Oxbridge Walk into Cambridge.

Wimpole Hall is the most spectacular eighteenth-century mansion house in Cambridgeshire. Built in 1640 for Sir Thomas Chicheley, the central hall has been extended and the existing building remodelled at various times and by various owners over the centuries. The interior provides a range of rooms and furnishings ranging from the Yellow Drawing Room, with its ornate ceiling, to the chapel designed by James Gibbs in the 1720s, with its "trompe l'oeil" murals depicting the Adoration of the Magi. Wimpole Hall reached the peak of its splendour in the time of the 4th Earl of Hardwicke

Wimpole Hall

and Queen Victoria and Prince Albert were entertained at a grand dinner and ball in 1843. Unfortunately, the profligate 5th Earl, known as "Champagne Charlie", was forced to sell the estate to pay his debts and the estate went into decline. Rudyard Kipling's daughter, Elsie Bainbridge, was the last private owner and when she died in 1976, she left the Wimpole estate to the National Trust.

The house is open from 1-5pm, end Mar to beginning Nov. It is closed Mon and Fri. On Bank Hol, Sun and Mon, it opens 11am-5pm. The restaurant opens 11am-5pm and serves lunches 12-2pm.

For further details (admission charges etc.) tel (01223) 207257.

Wimpole Park consists of 350 acres of parkland which has evolved over a long period and represents the work of a series of landscape architects and gardeners such as Bridgeman, Capability Brown and Humphrey Repton. Their diverse influences have resulted in the creation of an interesting park within which a series of walks link features such as the woodland belts, the lake and Chinese Bridge, and the folly, a ruin designed and built as such by Sanderson Miller, in 1771. A major difference in the appearance of the park today is due to the loss of the Great Avenue of Elms, which have been replaced by Limes. However, it will be many years before this aspect of the park can be restored to anything like its former glory. The park is open all the year round, from sunrise to sunset.

The Stableblock is the visitor reception with information and tickets. There are wagon rides to the farm and a landscape exhibition, tack and harness rooms, public telephone, guidebooks, etc. Open 10.30am-5pm, same days as the Hall.

Wimpole Home Farm is the largest Rare Breeds Centre in East Anglia and maintains a stock of farm animals no longer to be found on modern farms. In addition to being a working farm, there is a Victorian dairy and the eighteenth-century thatched barn houses a museum of farm machinery. Horse drawn wagons provide rides to the stableblock 12-5pm. There is also a gift shop and light refreshments are available.

Home Farm is open 10.30am-5pm, same days as the Hall.

AN OXBRIDGE WALK

GENERAL INFORMATION

En Route

Of particular interest	Cockayne Hatley church and churchyard
	Site of medieval village of Clopton
Accommodation	Nr Wrestlingworth (directly on line of march) -
	New England Farm (01767) 23247
	Nr Croydon (just below line of march) -
	Croydon House Farm (01767) 23207
	Arrington - Hardwicke Arms Hotel (01223) 208802
Camping	Croydon - back-packers/tents only
	Queen Adelaide pub (01223) 208278
Refreshments	Croydon - one pub
	Arrington - one pub
PO/shop	Arrington only
Public phone	Cockayne Hatley, Croydon, Arrington
Banks	None (nearest, Cambridge)
Parking	Roadside only

Wimpole Hall

Of particular interest	Wimpole Hall and Garden
	Wimpole Park (Chinese bridge, lake, folly)
	Wimpole Home Farm (rare breeds, museum)
Accommodation	Arrington - Hardwicke Arms Hotel (01223) 208802
	New Wimpole - Foxhounds, 71 Cambridge Rd
	(down avenue to A603) (01223) 207344
Refreshments	Hall restaurant, open 11am-5pm (lunch 12-2pm)
	Stableblock (light refreshments) 11am-5pm
PO/shop	National Trust shop (gifts and souvenirs)
Public phone	Yes - Stableblock
Bank	No
Parking	Free car park
Access	Road A603 (W of Cambridge)
	M11 (Junction 12)
	Rail As Cambridge
	Bus (01480) 463792, (01223) 423554

GAMLINGAY TO CAMBRIDGE

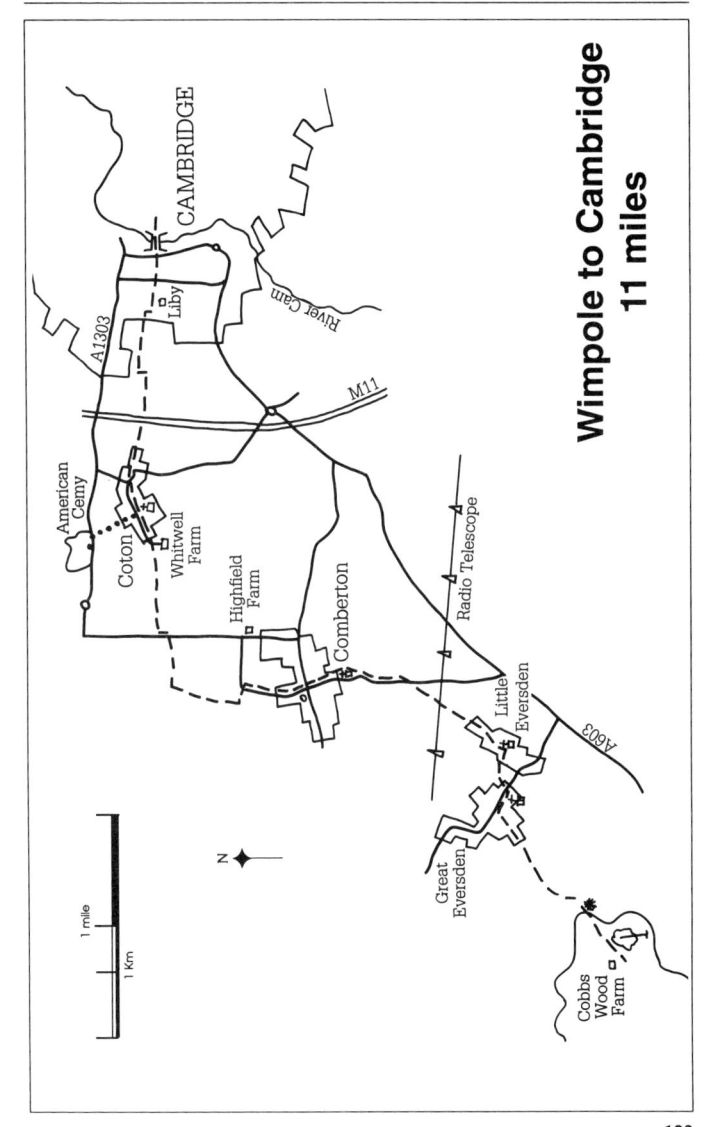

Wimpole to Cambridge
11 miles

AN OXBRIDGE WALK

WIMPOLE HALL - GREAT EVERSDEN - LITTLE EVERSDEN - COMBERTON - COTON - CAMBRIDGE - (11 miles)

Of particular interest

Cobbs Wood Farm Walk; views; radio telescope; Coton - American military cemetery; Cambridge.

After Wimpole Hall, this last section follows bridleway tracks and footpaths before picking up the Wimpole Way on the other side of Comberton.

From the T junction in Arrington, the Oxbridge route crosses diagonally left over the road and turns right through the ornamental iron gates opposite the almshouses built in 1846 for the Countess of Hardwicke. Inside the gates it follows the drive for half a mile across open parkland where cattle from the Rare Breeds Centre often graze. The drive continues past the south face of Wimpole Hall and keeps to the right of the Stableblock/visitors' centre. At the end of the car park behind the stable block, the route leaves on the left, via a wooden swing-gate next to a five-bar gate. From here the path crosses two pastures following way-marked oak-posts and heading for a swing-gate to the left of the red telephone box on the other side of the second field.

This path is part of a network of permissive paths (Woodland Walks) within Wimpole Park. In the unlikely event of it being closed, use the drive, which is a public right-of-way.

From the swing-gate, with Home Farm Rare Breeds Centre immediately to the left, the route crosses the road to follow a right-of-way along the farm-road opposite, labelled "Cobb's Wood Farm Walk".

The National Trust have made this attractive section of the route even more interesting by erecting noticeboards at intervals along the roadside which give details relating to the surrounding countryside, crops currently planted, farming methods, etc.

The route continues to follow the farm-road where it bears left after the single storey cottage with the large, central chimney, then across a bridge over a stream, and past the front of Cobb's Wood Farm and barns. After the farm the road becomes a well surfaced track winding uphill over open, arable farmland to the crest of the hill in front.

Two conveniently sited wooden benches almost at the top of the hill provide an opportunity to enjoy wide views across the 2400 acres of Wimpole Estate and the countryside to the south-east.

From the second bench on the left (which is where the Cobb's Wood Farm Walk leaves the route), the track continues ahead keeping to the left of a patch of young trees and small bushes, at the end of which it turns left along a headland path. In the left-hand corner of this large, arable field, the route emerges on the line of an ancient trackway known as the Mare Way.

The Mare Way follows the line of the escarpment with Eversden Wood, an SSSI to the left. This wood is one of the largest remaining areas of ash-maple type woodlands on chalky, boulder clay left in the County. The relatively high ground here also provides the last viewpoint along the Oxbridge route. To the north-east can be seen not only the array of dishes of the radio telescope, but also the first sight of the distant towers of the city of Cambridge.

The route crosses over to the right of the water tanks opposite and follows a wide track known as Wimpole Road which leads downhill to Merys Farm. Past the farm, the track becomes metalled, and eventually meets a road opposite The Hoops pub, formerly a

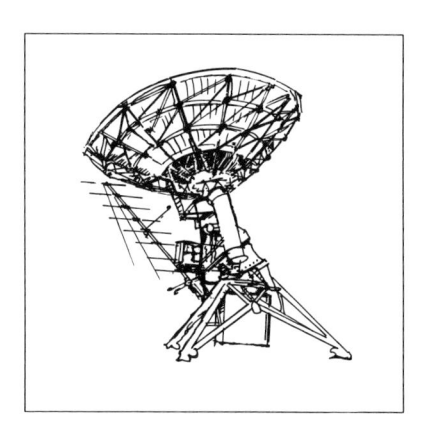

Radio telescope dish

Radio telescope dishes, Mullard Observatory

smithy in the village of Great Eversden.

B+B accommodation is available in the village at The Moat House, opposite the PO/shop along the road to the left.

The route turns right, along the roadside path, to St Mary's church (1636). Just past the church, on the opposite side of the road, it leaves the road via a metal swing-gate to follow a path across a small field. The path then becomes metalled and continues through a series of swing-gates, past a small playing field on the right and crossing over a narrow lane next to Five Gables Farmhouse, a former medieval hall-house. A short distance further on it meets and turns left along the High Street of Little Eversden. It follows the road past a large, thatched barn on the left, and continues ahead past the school on the right which stands on the corner of the lane leading to the church. The High Street eventually becomes "Lowfields" and, where the houses end, the route continues ahead on a track over arable fields. A white post on the left-hand side of the track marks where the route crosses the old railway line along which the radio telescope dishes are now sited.

The Cavendish Laboratory, Cambridge University, built the Mullard Radio Astronomy Observatory on a site previously owned by the Ministry of Defence. During the war this area was part of a huge ammunition and bomb dump serving nearby airfields. Today, the old railway lines and sidings serve a more peaceful purpose as linear sites for the radio telescope aerials and dishes which look as alien in their rural surroundings as the Cardington Airship sheds in Bedfordshire.

On the other side of the old railway line, the path continues along the line of a hedge and ditch before crossing a field diagonally right to the road, where the route turns left. After about half a mile, just after the road bends right, then left, the route turns right along Church Lane for the short distance leading to St Mary's church. Through the churchyard and to the rear of the church a cobbled way leads past a very large farm house down to a roadside path which runs from here to the crossroads at the centre of the village of Comberton.

Comberton once had an ancient 50ft maze which was given into the care of the village school but which subsequently disappeared - believed built over when the school expanded.

The route crosses straight over the crossroads, with the village sign and duck pond on the left, into Green End and continues ahead (B+B accommodation available at 'The Moat House' on the left-hand side of the road) for about a quarter of a mile. Just before the road turns sharply right, the route leaves the road on the left where a finger-post indicates a track to Hardwick.

For the last campsite on the route before Cambridge, follow the road right for a short distance to where it meets another road. The campsite entrance is across the road, to the right - beware maniac motorists on this long stretch of straight road!

From the finger-post the track follows the hedge-line and then turns right, between hedges, up a long rise, at the top of which the Oxbridge route joins the Wimpole Way. From here the route is way-marked as for the Wimpole Way.

At the top of the rise the route keeps to the right of the woods known as Starve Goose Plantation and then turns right down to the road where it turns left. About half way up the hill ahead the way-marked Wimpole Way turns right along an ancient track known as Whitwell Way. Once clear of the woods and hedges, the track continues across open, arable fields with the square tower of Cambridge University library now clearly visible ahead. Where the

AN OXBRIDGE WALK

tall hedges resume on both sides of the track for a short distance a danger sign refers to the rifle range on the other side of a hill to the right. Eventually, the last few yards of a concrete drive to Whitwell Farm (B+B accommodation available) is reached, after which a road leads straight ahead into Coton.

A short distance along the road, on the left hand side, is the village school. To the left of the school a footpath, signposted Madingley Hill, can be followed for the the half mile up the hill to the main road, on the other side of which is the American Forces Cemetery.

Highly recommended visit - American Military Cemetery and Memorial

The cemetery and memorial was established here because a large proportion of American casualties, many of whom were members of the United States Army Air Corps, occurred in this general area of East Anglia. Inside the main entrance and in front of the Visitors' Building, stands a 72ft flagpole, from which radiate the gravestones of the 3812 American War Dead. To the east, the Great Mall with its reflecting pools is flanked on one side by the Wall of the Missing, which records the names and particulars of the 5125 missing in action. Along the wall are four statues representing a soldier, a sailor, an airman and a coast guard. At the end of the Great Mall is the memorial which, like the great wall, is built of Portland stone.

The map on the south, exterior wall, was executed in the workshop of David Kindersley, an English artist, and indicates sites lent to the United States in preparation and support of military operations. The interior of the Memorial is divided into a large museum chamber and a smaller devotional chapel. The map, "The Mastery of the Atlantic - The Great Assault", was designed by the American artist Herbert Gute. The mosaic ceiling, by American artist Francis Scott Bradford, is a memorial to those Americans who gave their lives while serving in the USAAF.

Before leaving the cemetery, so close to your journey's end, be sure to read the inscription on the base of the flagpole, taken from John McCrae's poem In Flanders' Fields.

From the cemetery the route is re-traced back down the hill to the school where it turns left along the road, past the church and through the village.

Coton is of Saxon origins and its church, St Peter's, dates from the twelfth century when Coton was a hamlet in the parish of Grantchester. Amongst many notable features in the church is a twelfth-century Saxon font, two small Norman windows in the chancel and a memorial to Andrew Downes, Regius Professor of Greek and one of the translators of the King James Bible, who died in 1627.

Past the church, at a T junction, the route turns right along the road as far as the Plough pub where it turns left at the fork along a narrow road called "The Footpath", with houses on the left and a large green and playing fields to the right. At the end of the houses (B+B accommodation available at 57, The Footpath) the road becomes a metalled path and cycleway which continues all the way from here for the remaining 2 miles or so to the outskirts of Cambridge. After negotiating the last footbridge over the last motorway (M11), the path runs more or less straight ahead with the tower of the university library now looking very close. Eventually, the path runs past the Cavendish Laboratories, only to be greeted at the time of writing by the all-too-familiar roar of bulldozers eating into a dwindling green-belt. Only small comfort can be derived from the fact that at least it's not yet another supermarket, since the site is being developed as a new athletics centre for the University of Cambridge. Nevertheless:

> *All fields we'll turn to sports grounds, lit at night*
> *From concrete standards by fluorescent light:*
> *And over all the land, instead of trees,*
> *Clean poles and wire will whisper in the breeze.*
> *We'll keep one ancient village just to show*
> *What England once was when the times were slow -*

Extract from, The Town Clerk's Views
by John Betjeman

Where the path meets the road the route crosses straight over to follow Adam Road at the end of which it crosses over a main road and continues along a metalled path signposted "City Centre", known as Burrell's Walk, which eventually passes the university library and tower, which has been seen in the distance all day. Across a last main road, the route carries on ahead down Garret Hostel Lane leading to the only bridge over the college "Backs", which is a public right-of-way.

Garret Hostel Bridge, River Cam, Cambridge

Here, the Oxbridge Walk ends as it began, at a bridge over a river. Having started at Folly Bridge over the Thames next to Christ Church, it ends at the Cam in Cambridge with Trinity College and St John's College to the left of Garret Hostel Lane bridge, Clare College and King's College to the right.

The 115 mile journey through the secret heart of England, linking the two most prestigious university cities in the country, is over - but the best is still to come, as all the glories of Cambridge lie before you!

Those for whom this is their first visit to the city are, therefore, to be envied - but to be envied most are those who have completed the Oxbridge Walk and who are returning to their Alma Mater, Cambridge, because they are coming home.

GAMLINGAY TO CAMBRIDGE

GENERAL INFORMATION

En Route

Of particular interest	Cobbs Wood Farm Walk
	Views
	Radio telescope
	Coton - American military cemetery
Accommodation	Great Eversden - The Moat House (01223) 262836
	Comberton - The Moat House (01223) 263978
	- 28 West St (01223) 262914
	Coton - Whitwell Farm (01954) 210453
	- 57 The Footpath (May/Sept) (01954) 210455
	American military cemetery - Woodfield House (200yds left) (01954) 210265
Camping	Comberton - Highfield Farm
	(Five-star camping park) (01223) 262308
Refreshments	Great Eversden - one pub
	Comberton - two pubs
	Coton - two pubs
PO/shop	Great Eversden - Yes
	Comberton - PO/shop, small supermarket, late shop, butchers
	Coton - Yes
Public phone	Great Eversden, Comberton, Coton
Banks	None - nearest, Cambridge
Parking	Great Eversden - field behind village hall
	Comberton - off-road only
	Coton - off-road plus short term parking at recreation ground.

Cambridge City (See Introduction)

AN OXBRIDGE WALK

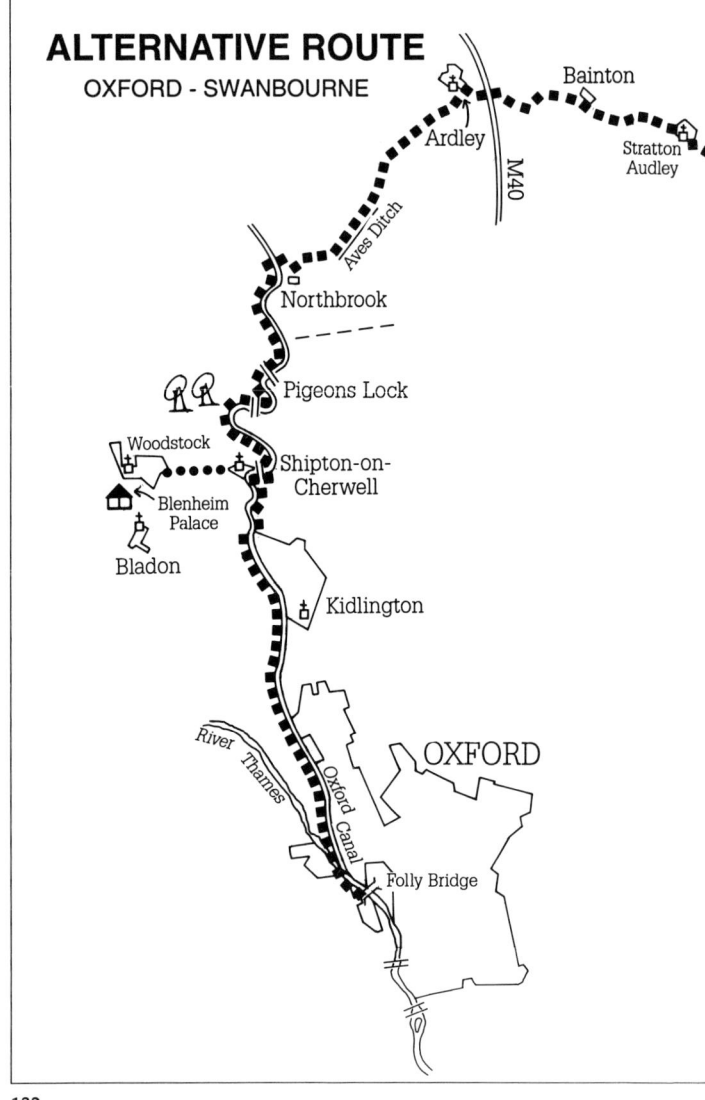

ALTERNATIVE ROUTE
OXFORD - SWANBOURNE

Bainton
Ardley
Stratton Audley
M40
Aves Ditch
Northbrook
Pigeons Lock
Woodstock
Shipton-on-Cherwell
Blenheim Palace
Bladon
Kidlington
River Thames
Oxford Canal
OXFORD
Folly Bridge

ALTERNATIVE ROUTE - OXFORDSHIRE

42 Miles

Alternative Route - Oxfordshire
Oxford - (Visit Woodstock, Blenheim Palace) -
Stratton Audley: (25 miles excl. visit)

OXFORD (via Oxford Canal) - SHIPTON ON CHERWELL -
PIGEON LOCK - (11 miles)

Of particular interest

Oxford
Oxford Canal - locks; narrow boats.
Detour - Woodstock; church; County Museum; Blenheim Palace; Bladon church (Churchill's grave).

The alternative route for the first third of the Oxbridge Walk travels north out of the city of Oxford following the Oxford Canal. It includes an optional

Isis House, Folly Bridge

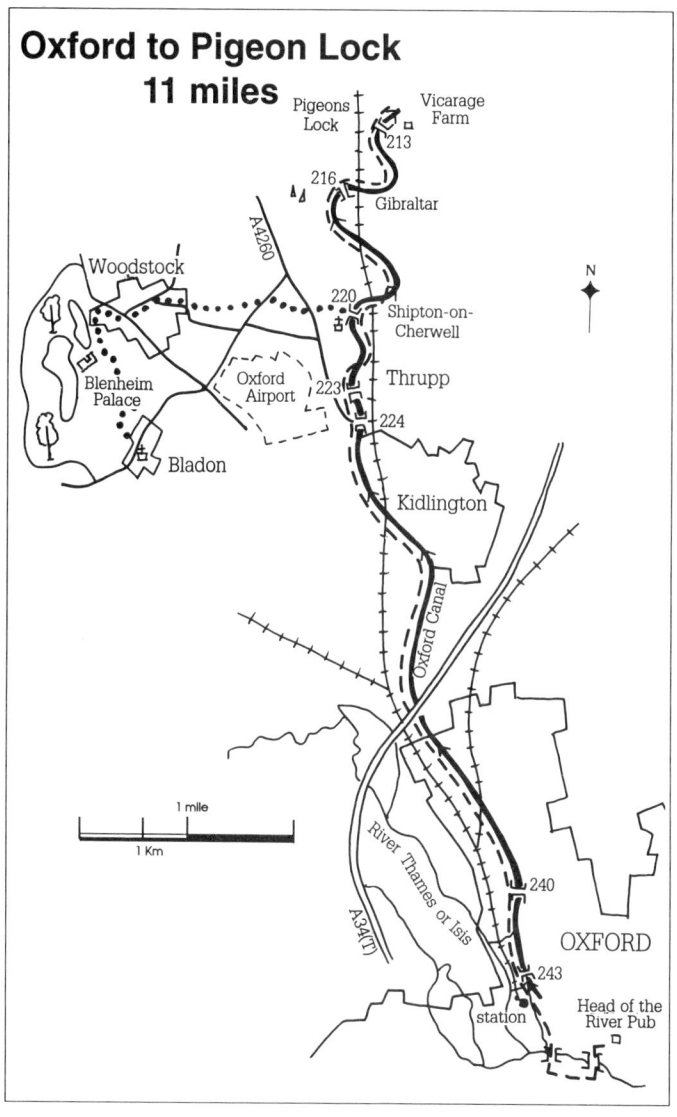

ALTERNATIVE ROUTE - OXFORDSHIRE

Oxford to Pigeon Lock
11 miles

visit to Blenheim Palace on its itinerary, after which it traverses countryside less well known, although generally no less attractive, than the southern route. Used in conjunction with the main route it could also provide a very interesting circular walk of about 80 miles travelling either north or south from Oxford.

At the bottom of Aldgate is the Head of the River pub, where both routes of the Oxbridge Walk begin. From the pub the northern route crosses to the other side of the road and then across Folly Bridge over the Thames. The bridge is partly built on an island, which the river divides to flow either side of, and the Thames-side path leaves on the right, after crossing the second of the two channels. From the bridge the path first angles down to the riverbank opposite Isis House, with its ornate facade of statuettes and metal balconies.

From here it continues upstream, along the bank past the pleasant but unpretentious houses in Jubiliee Terrace, which compare favourably with the modern, up-market town-houses and flats on the river's opposite bank. After passing under an iron girder footbridge, the first glimpse of open countryside ahead reinforces an atmosphere of almost rural tranquillity, not often found this close to a city centre. Further along, an iron, ex-railway bridge is reached, and it is here that the route leaves the main channel of the Thames in order to follow one of its branches through to the start of the Oxford Canal. The route crosses over the bridge and descends stone steps on the other side from where it turns left and then right along the right-hand side of this branch of the Thames. At the end of the houses on the right, with the ice-rink to the left, the route crosses over Thames Street and through Abbey Place car park in front of the Oxford College of Further Education. The path continues from the corner of the car park next to the river, which it follows to where it meets Paradise Street.

To the right along Paradise Street is Paradise Square, overlooked by the walls of Oxford prison - for those prisoners looking down on this street and square from between bars, it really is a case of Paradise lost!

The route turns left along Paradise Street, over a bridge crossing the river, then bends right to follow the river past St George's Tower which, together with the mound overlooking Nuffield College in New Road, is all that remains of the castle built about 1071. Ignoring

Quaking Bridge(!) on the right, the route follows the path, which has switched to the left-hand side of the river, along Lower Fisher Row. The path continues ahead, crossing Park End Street, (turn left for Oxford railway station), before arriving at Hythe Bridge (1821), with the Antiquity Hall pub on the left. Here the route crosses to the other side of the road and turns right over the bridge, on the other side of which a path leads down to what is now the start of the Oxford Canal.

The Oxford Canal is one of the oldest in the country and was completed in 1790. James Brindley surveyed the line of the canal which linked Oxford with Coventry thereby providing, via the Thames, a continuous waterway between Birmingham and London. During the nineteenth century it was an important route into the city for timber, coal, lime and stone, and loading wharves once extended under the road just crossed to the area which is now a large car park in front of Nuffield College. The Oxford Canal is a contour canal and wanders through the countryside to the north of Oxford, often entwined with the River Cherwell which it actually joins for one short stretch.

The canal and tow-path provide a refuge for a surprising range of wildlife which thrives in spite of canal users. Birds such as linnet, finches and kingfishers are not uncommon, whilst water-fowl are commonplace. In the adjoining water-meadows plants such as ox-eye daisies, meadow buttercups, lady's bedstraw, meadow sweet, greater willowherb and yellow flag abound in season. Insect life is prolific in the damp conditions with dragonflies more numerous than the ducks in summer.

The tow-path is in generally good condition and is due to be upgraded by the summer of 1995 when the Waterways Board plans to designate the Oxford Canal as the third of their official, long distance, canalside footpaths. The first such walk was along the Grand Union Canal, crossed by the Oxbridge Walk at the end of the Cross Bucks Way. The second, the Kennet and Avon Canal in the summer of 1994.

From Hythe Bridge the path follows the left-hand side of the canal, sandwiched between the river and the canal and with the gardens and playing fields of Worcester College on the right behind a screen of trees. This end of the canal is crowded with traditional narrow-boats converted into house-boats but within a short distance the path reaches Isis Lock, which could now be said to be where the canal really starts.

Ironwork Bridge, Isis Lock, Oxford Canal

The river, known as the Isis or "Old Thames", turns to the left and provides navigable access from the lock to the main channel of the River Thames.

The path continues over a distinctive black and white wrought iron bridge (No243) and along the left-hand bank of the canal past a large boatyard on the opposite bank, dominated by the tower of St Barnabas Church.

This noted Catholic Anglican church, which originally looked down on coaling wharves, was inspired by the church at Torcello in Venice and was designed by Sir Arthur Blomfield in the 1860s. In its turn it was also the inspiration for the church of "St Silas" in Thomas Hardy's book Jude the Obscure.

Further along, the tow-path passes Lucy's Iron Works, also on the opposite bank, a dismal, dark and clangorous reminder of the canal's more industrial past.

Today, the canal is surprisingly secluded and almost rural in spite of its closeness to the city and its suburbs along this stretch. The main interest for the next mile or so continues to lie in the opposite bank, where the back gardens of suburbia run down to the canal. Each garden passed reveals something about its owners. An Englishman's home may be his castle, and from the outside his "castle" might look the same as most others, but his back garden often tells an altogether different story!

On the road, just off Bridge 240, there is a post office, stores and off-licence. Further along, the tow-path passes the first of the wooden, manually operated and counter-balanced lift bridges so attractively in keeping with the style and scale of this canal. After the railway bridge and Wolvercote Lock, the canal passes under a series of road bridges to reach more open country and Duke's Cut and Lock, which provides access to the Thames and allows waterborne traffic to by-pass Oxford. Above the lock the canal continues northwards under another road bridge and then traverses lightly wooded fields and meadows.

The stretch of canal from here to Kidlington Green Lock is surprisingly good for bird-spotting and kingfishers are not uncommon. The canal then skirts the western edge of Kidlington, the last outpost of suburbia, before running under a railway bridge and through an industrial estate, on the other side of which it meets the busy A423 at Bridge 224, next to The Wise Alderman pub.

From here the canal runs alongside the road past Bridge 223, and The Jolly Boatman. Further along, "The Boat" is followed by a row of attractive canalside cottages above which the tow-path reaches Thrupp Lock and a British Waterways maintenance yard.

A number of conveniently sited benches around the edge of the basin above the lock provide an ideal resting place from which to contemplate this wider stretch of canal. North from here the canal follows the Cherwell Valley and the river is never very far away. As a result, the canal tends to meander almost as much as the river and the two actually become one for the best part of a mile.

From here the tow-path keeps to the right-hand side of the canal with the river running virtually alongside the other side of the path until the river branches away shortly before reaching the church on the opposite bank and Bridge 220, which gives access to the village of Shipton-on-Cherwell.

From here, those who wish to include Woodstock and Blenheim Palace in their itinerary leave, and return, via the bridge over the canal. Those who do not wish make this visit carry on up the canal - refer to the directions headed "Main Route"below.

Highly recommended visit - Woodstock, Blenheim Palace and the grave of Sir Winston Churchill (2 miles each way out and back on the same route)

The route for Woodstock turns left, over the canal bridge, and continues up the road ahead past the church and up the side of Shipton House. At the T junction the route again follows the road ahead along the roadside path. At the main road it crosses slightly to the right to pick up a field path on the other side.

If this path is not marked across the crop, stay with the hedge on the left until reaching the next road. Light aircraft activity in this area is associated with Oxford Airport to the south, the main training base in Britain for future airline pilots.

The path crosses a wide field and a small stream before climbing up a steep bank to meet a road which the route crosses over and turns left along the broad grass verge for about a hundred yards.

Just before the road bends, the path turns right over a ditch and then a stile set well back from the road. From here the path leads to a gap in the hedge next to a metal gate and then heads diagonally left across a wide, arable field. From a stile in the hedge next to a sycamore tree, a fenced-in path becomes a headland path before crossing another arable field on the other side of which a road leads straight ahead into Woodstock.

Woodstock was of historical importance long before the building of Blenheim Palace. A favourite manor and hunting lodge for English Kings, it has royal associations dating back to the time of Alfred the Great. Edward of Woodstock, the Black Prince, was born here in 1330 and Woodstock remained a royal manor until the reign of Queen Anne.

Today, it is a small, attractive town with many Georgian houses and shops. The County Museum, with the town stocks outside, is housed in the sixteenth-century Fletcher's House. Hostelleries such as the famous Bear Hotel, reputed to have been first licensed in 1232, cater for the many tourists who flock here in the high season. It is advisable, therefore, to book accommodation with the Woodstock Tourist information office in advance: (01993) 811038.

From the end of Park Street, a triumphal arch leads to one of the most famous views in England, Blenheim Palace next to the Grand Bridge seen across the park and lake.

ALTERNATIVE ROUTE - OXFORDSHIRE

Visitors' Gates, Blenheim Palace, Woodstock

Blenheim Palace is included on UNESCO's World Heritage List as a site of special Heritage Value. Historically, the manor of Woodstock was given by Queen Anne, on behalf of a grateful nation, to John Churchill, 1st Duke of Marlborough, following his famous victory over the French at Blenheim. John Vanbrugh was commissioned to build the Palace which took over 20 years to complete and resulted in the creation of a Baroque masterpiece covering 7 acres (the country's largest house), set in 2200 acres (880 hectares) of parkland landscaped by Capability Brown. The lakes provided the first broad areas of permanent water in Oxfordshire and have been well colonised by birds.

The Palace has many magnificent state rooms which contain the famous Blenheim tapestries and countless other treasures. There is also an exhibition commemorating the life of Winston Churchill, grandson of the 8th Duke, which includes manuscripts, paintings, personal belongings, books, photographs, letters and a unique photographic collage covering the period of his life.

In addition to the Palace, there is a Pleasure Gardens complex and it is worth crossing the Grand Bridge for a closer look at the lake and the Column of Victory. Looking back towards the Palace from its proud base, which records details of the Duke's victory, one cannot fail to be impressed, if not overwhelmed, by the sheer scale and grandeur of it all.

A number of special events are organised throughout the year, from laser and firework displays which accompany classical music concerts, to the well-known International Horse Trials.

The Palace is open daily, from 10.30am-5.30pm, mid-March-end Oct. The Park is open daily, 9am-4.45pm throughout the year.

For further details (admission charges, etc.) tel (01993) 811325.

Sir Winston Churchill's Grave is in St Martin's churchyard, Bladon, and provides an opportunity to pay your respects to a hero of more recent times. From the Palace the route to Bladon follows the road past the Pleasure Gardens and turns right at the crossroads. It then forks left at the lodge and continues on a road leading down to an iron gate from where a road leads ahead into the village of Bladon. At the main road the route crosses over to the left and enters the churchyard where the Spencer-Churchill family graves are located close to the tower of St Martin's church.

Buried with his family, the unadorned grave of the nation's wartime leader is in moving contrast to the opulence of Blenheim Palace. The casual, unassuming ordinariness of this, the grave that he chose for himself, comes at first as something of a shock. It is only after quiet contemplation that an understanding is reached of how his grave, by its simplicity and its very English disdain for "making a fuss", is, indeed, a fitting tribute to a very great Englishman.

After visiting Blenheim Palace and Woodstock, the same route is re-traced, back to the canal.

Main Route

Above Shipton-on-Cherwell the canal keeps ever closer company with the Cherwell across wide water-meadows that regularly flood each winter.

Winter brings its own opportunities for "twitchers" and fishers - herons, swans and seabirds haunt the flooded water-meadows, whilst both the river and canal offer first class fishing for roach, pike and chub.

About a quarter of a mile above Shipton-on-Cherwell, the tow-path passes under a railway bridge which was the scene of a tragic disaster on Christmas Eve 1874.

On this night, nine carriages fell from the bridge onto the frozen ice below and 34 people were killed. Some were buried in nearby Hampton Gay churchyard, including the bodies of two children that were never claimed.

The canal swings back in a north-easterly direction and, at Shipton Weir Lock, the tow-path crosses to the left-hand bank just before the canal and the River Cherwell join to form one waterway for about a mile.

The tall chimney at the quarry and huge cement works on Bunker Hill dominates this end of the valley for several miles.

After passing under the railway again, the path crosses over a black and white iron girder footbridge where the river and canal part company. Up to the next lock there is a good view of the dishes of the nearby satellite earth station and, further on, the canal turns in a more easterly direction before running under Bridge 216.

The Rock of Gibraltar pub, 1787, set above the canal to the right, has an interesting and wide-ranging collection of memorabilia including a restored dog turn-spit above an open hearth.

Past Enslow, the canal wanders under the railway yet again

AN OXBRIDGE WALK

heading in an overall north-easterly direction through undulating, wooded countryside and, eventually, arrives at Pigeon Lock.

B+B is available at nearby Vicarage Farm. Cross over the canal, via the bridge, and turn left on Mill Lane. A few yards up from the bend to the bridge a wooden, five-bar gate gives access to a farm-track leading to the rear of the farm. Alternatively, B+B can be found at Tackley, a mile north-west of Pigeon Lock across the Cherwell - take the footpath down the left-hand side of the first house.

PIGEON LOCK - NORTHBROOK - ARDLEY - BAINTON - STRATTON AUDLEY - (14 miles)

Of particular interest
Oxford Canal; Aves Ditch; Bainton, monument to "Lady".

The tow-path continues on the left-hand side of the canal, with the river often in close company on the same side, for 2 miles up to Dashwood Lock. Here, Bridge 209 gives access to the right-hand bank and the Oxbridge route finally leaves the canal. Neither Northbrook Lock nor the bridge that follows it have access to public rights-of-way.

Having crossed Bridge 209 and turned right through a farm-gate, the path runs diagonally right across the field and up to a wooden swing-gate in the top corner next a small wood (Northbrook Spinney). From here the route turns right along a track which runs to the left of a small cottage and through another swing-gate to turn left on a small lane.

The lane runs through the isolated hamlet of Northbrook, where horse races held as early as 1718 were once an important social event that helped to bring prosperity to the nearby market-town of Bicester.

On reaching a terrace of cottages on the left, the route turns left, up the side of the first cottage, on a bridle-track which runs uphill and straight across the road at the top. From here it continues ahead across a wide, arable field, almost on the other side of which it keeps to the right of a small wood. In the corner of the field it meets a cross tracks where it turns left on a path which follows the line of Aves Ditch.

ALTERNATIVE ROUTE - OXFORDSHIRE

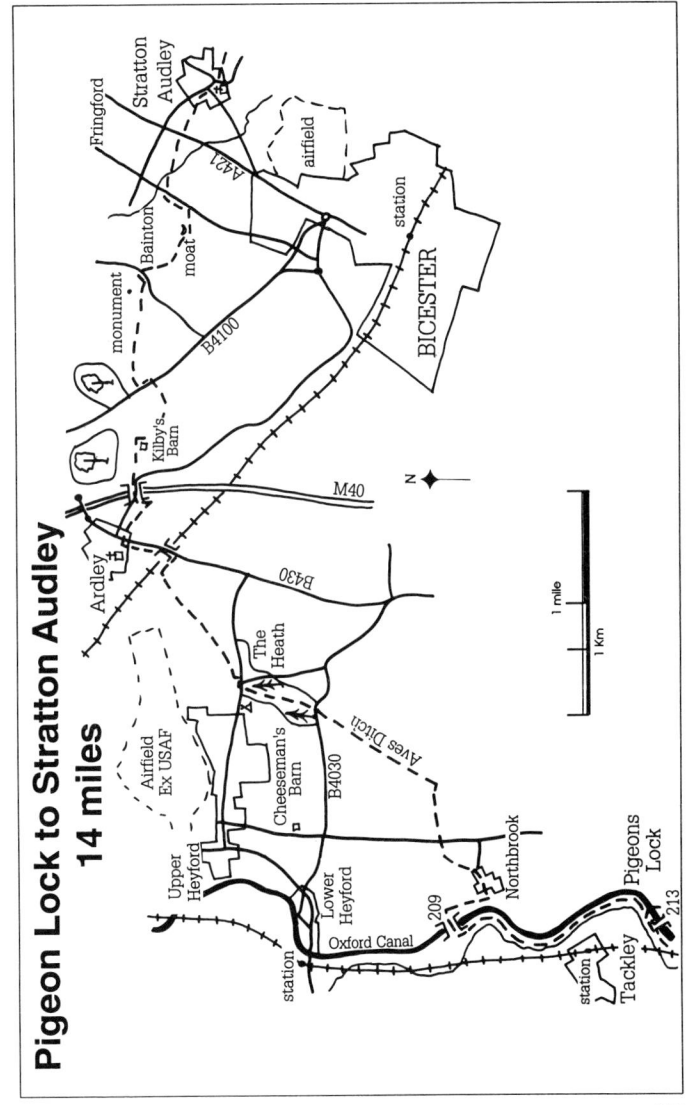

Aves Ditch runs for about 3 miles in a north-easterly direction and its origins and purpose are so old as to remain a mystery. It may have been a pre-Saxon tribal boundary, possibly dating back as far as the second or third century. All that is known for certain is that reference is made to it in 1396 and it occurs earlier as Aves Ditch Way.

For a short distance from where it turned left at the cross-tracks, the path is narrow and hemmed in by high hedges and undergrowth. However, it soon broadens out where it turns left to follow the course of a good track to the right of the ditch for about a mile. Hedges and trees, including the occasional Scots pine, border the ditch. Together with the beech trees on the right an avenue provides very pleasant walking conditions and a corridor which acts as a refuge for wildlife across this arable landscape.

Just before the road ahead is reached, the path switches to the left-hand side of the hedge and ditch from where it carries on through a gap on the left-hand side of a metal gate. From here it runs straight over the road to continue ahead through a wood mainly consisting of tightly packed conifers alive with game birds. Half way through the wood, the track dog-legs to the right of the hedge in front and continues ahead to another road at a Y junction.

There is a campsite and shop a few hundred yards down the road to the left. The nearest B+B is at Cheeseman's Barn, just over a mile past the campsite; turn left along Kirtlington Road.

The route crosses the road in front and turns right along the road signposted to Ardley. After a few hundred yards, it turns left across an arable field on a bridleway finger-posted to the same village. Through a swing-gate on the other side of the field the route turns right and stays with the hedge as it turns right and left for the next few fields.

To the left can plainly be seen the blast-proof bomb and missile stores on the perimeter of what was, until very recently, the home of the 20th Fighter Wing, USAF. The F111s of the "Fighting Fifty-Fifth" have gone, and the thunder of their engines will not be missed by local inhabitants. However, the departure of the 'planes means that the Americans who flew and serviced them, together with the ground crews and support personnel that manned the base have also gone - and they, and their money, will be sadly missed locally. In addition, some of the proposed, alternative uses currently under consideration for this now vacant site may make its use as

ALTERNATIVE ROUTE - OXFORDSHIRE

an air base seem almost attractive by comparison!

Past a small plantation of newly planted trees, the path turns right through one metal farm-gate then almost immediately left through another. From here the path runs ahead on a barely distinguishable track across a wide pasture, through another gate and continues ahead keeping to the right of the fence. Eventually, at a corner, it crosses an open ditch and goes through a swing gate and is way-marked to the right, along the hedge-line (although the OS PF map shows it carrying straight over the field). The path follows the hedge to the corner of the field where it turns left along the hedge-line which it stays with for some distance to where a swing gate takes it right, along the embankment of a railway line. At the road, the route turns left, over the railway bridge, and, after a few hundred yards, along a roadside path leading up to the Fox and Hounds pub opposite the church in the small village of Ardley.

Ardley and Fewcott now form one village joined together by substantial, modern developments. Close to the partly Norman church are some earthworks which mark the site and all that is left of a small castle. The closure of the nearby American airbase must have been a considerable relief to people living here since the village and a nearby nature reserve were almost directly under the approach to the main runway.

The route turns right from the road at a finger-posted footpath just before the pub. For the first hundred yards or so it keeps to the right of the hedge, but then switches to the other side over a fence closing a gap next to a small oak tree. From here it continues along the hedge-line in the same direction until a stile on the right takes it back to the other side of the hedge again. The path carries on along the hedge to where it meets the M40 motorway where it turns left through the first of a series of metal swing-gates up to the road.

The route turns right along the road and over the bridge across the motorway, on the other side of which a way-marked bridle-path to the left leads along a farm-track. After a short distance, the track turns right and then keeps on ahead until a junction of tracks in front of a collection of barns. Here the route goes ahead between a corrugated iron shed and substantial stone barn (look for the blue, bridleway arrow on the end of the shed). The path turns right down the side of the barn and continues as a headland track keeping to the left of the hedge. At a T junction, it turns right on a well used track and then left at the next junction following the hedge to another road.

The route turns left to follow the road up the rise for about a quarter of a mile, before turning right, over a footbridge along a bridleway finger-posted to Bainton. After passing between two wooden posts, the path continues ahead keeping to the left of the hedge across a long, arable field at the top corner of which it runs through a narrow belt of scrubby woodland. After about a hundred yards, a gateway leads to a path which continues ahead along the hedge for the next few fields. Eventually, the path turns left, over a footbridge, and then right on a farm-track to the rear of a wood-yard on the outskirts of Bainton.

Across the field on the left can be seen a 20ft high granite obelisk built in commemoration of a favourite fox-hound and inscribed as follows: "Erected in 1812 by Sir Thomas Mostyn Bart, MP. MFH Bicester Hounds 1800 to 1830. In memory of his favourite hound 'Lady'".

The track continues ahead past some grain silos and then a large stone barn at the end of which it turns right down through a metal farm-gate to reach the lane in the centre of the hamlet of Bainton.

Bainton is another small, isolated, rural hamlet. In the past more happened here than just farming, as it once provided the kennels for the Bicester hunt, but Lady's memorial is all that survives as a reminder of Bainton's former glories.

At the lane the route turns left for a short distance, then right at a finger-post indicating a bridleway to Moat Farm along the farm-road leading to Home Farm. After passing barns on the right, the bridleway is way-marked through two metal farm-gates. After the gates, the path bears right across a meadow and past a stone barn to another gate in the right-hand corner of the field. From here, it turns left along the hedge-line then through a gate next to a small pond fed by a weed filled stream. The path continues ahead, heading for a wooden swing-gate in the far hedge, after which it continues along the hedge-line to the farmhouse of Moat Farm. The path turns right to skirt the moat surrounding the house on three sides, before turning right on a concrete track running down to the road.

Here, the route turns left and, after a few hundred yards along the road, right where a newly installed finger-post indicates a path running diagonally left across the corner of an arable field, then over a new footbridge into the rough pasture behind Cotmore House. The path then passes a small stone barn as it crosses to the edge of the woods at the back of the house. From here it continues ahead, roughly parallel with the stream on the right, to a gateway. Across rough pasture in front the path aims to the left of the nearest electricity pole, heading for a small wooden gate in the far hedge.

The route crosses over the busy main road and, from a roadside stile, the path continues to the right of the hedge in front down the length of a long field. Almost in the corner of the field it crosses a wide, grassy track and turns left, over the fence. From here the path crosses a small paddock to a stile next to a white gate and then diagonally right to another new footbridge leading to the road. The route turns right along the road and over the cross-roads into Stratton Audley. After passing the Red Lion pub, the route turns right at the road junction by the church and follows the road for about 50 yards to where the Cross Bucks Way leaves on the left via a way-marked stile.

Stratton Audley is an attractive village whose grey stone buildings clustered around the church and the pub form as pretty a picture as any likely to be seen in Oxfordshire. The village was connected with the noble Audley family who built a castle here in the Middle Ages, although nothing has survived except a few mounds in a field near the church. The church is mainly fourteenth and fifteenth century and has large late medieval windows. Note especially the Borlase Tomb, south of the chancel, a magnificent Baroque monument to an actor attired in the costume of a Roman Legionary complete with periwig! B+B is available at the Old School in the village.

GENERAL INFORMATION - OXFORDSHIRE

Oxford See Introduction

En Route

Of particular interest Oxford Canal
Woodstock, County Museum

AN OXBRIDGE WALK

	Blenheim Palace
	Bladon church (Churchill's grave)
	Aves Ditch
Accommodation	Woodstock - Tourist Info Centre (01993) 811038
	Near Pigeon Lock - Vicarage Farm (01869) 50254
	Tackley - Harborne House (01869) 83496
	Upper Heyford - Dee-dees cottage
	Cheeseman's Barn (01869) 232396
	Stratton Audley - The Old School (01869) 277371
Camping	Leys Farm Mobile Home Park, Camp Rd, Upper Heyford (01869) 232048
Refreshments	Oxford Canal - Kidlington - The Wise Alderman, Bridge 224
	Thrupp - Canalside, The Boat & Jolly Boatman, Bridge 223
	Rock of Gibraltar, Bridge 216
	Ardley - one pub
	Stratton Audley - one pub
Campsite shop	Camp Rd, Upper Heyford (as above)
Public phone	Thrupp, Shipton-on-Cherwell,
	Ardley, Stratton Audley
Banks	Nearest, Woodstock
Parking	Woodstock - free car-park
	Northbrook - off-road parking
	Ardley - roadside only
Tourist information	Woodstock - Hensington Road (01993) 811038
Misc	Woodstock - swimming pool; cycle hire
Access to Canal	Road A4260/A4095 N of Oxford
	Rail Oxford City Station
	Tackley Station/Upper Heyford Station (01865) 722333
	Bus (01865) 711312
Access to Woodstock	Road A44 NW of Oxford
	Rail As Oxford
	Bus (01865) 772250
Access to Stratton Audley	Road A42 NE Bicester
	Rail nearest station, Bicester
	(London/Banbury) (01494) 441561
	(Oxford/Bicester) (01865) 722333
	Bus (01295) 768292

> *Alternative Route - Buckinghamshire*
> *Stratton Audley (Oxfordshire border) -*
> *Swanbourne (Buckinghamshire): 17 miles*

STRATTON AUDLEY - POUNDON - TWYFORD - HILLESDEN - (8 miles)

Of particular interest

Poundon Hill (view); Twyford church; Three Bridge Mill; Hillesden church - the "Cathedral in the Fields".

From Stratton Audley the route follows the way-marked Cross Bucks Way.

The route leaves opposite the churchyard, where the houses end on the left. From here, a waymarked finger-post indicates the start of the Cross Bucks Way. Over a stile the path follows a hedge across a small pasture which clearly shows the remains of an ancient moat to the right. From a stile in the corner, it continues ahead keeping to the right of a fence and hedge on a headland path. It then crosses two more stiles separated by a few yards and followed by a footbridge. The path continues to follow the hedge down a long field before reaching another footbridge and stile, from where it runs diagonally left over an arable field and across a footbridge over a wide ditch. The route turns right along the ditch for a few yards, and then left, keeping to the left of the hedge. The path now follows the hedge round a large, arable field to eventually arrive at a way-marked post before crossing a footbridge and stile. From here the path crosses the field aiming at its top right-hand corner, next to a gap in the hedge, and turns right, over a stile partly concealed by the hedge. Keeping to the left of the wire fence, it then passes a small plantation of newly planted trees to arrive at a stile, from where the path crosses a farm-track and continues ahead over a double stile and footbridge. It then bears right, over a wide pasture, on the other side of which a stile takes it to the road.

Stratton Audley to Hillesden
8 miles

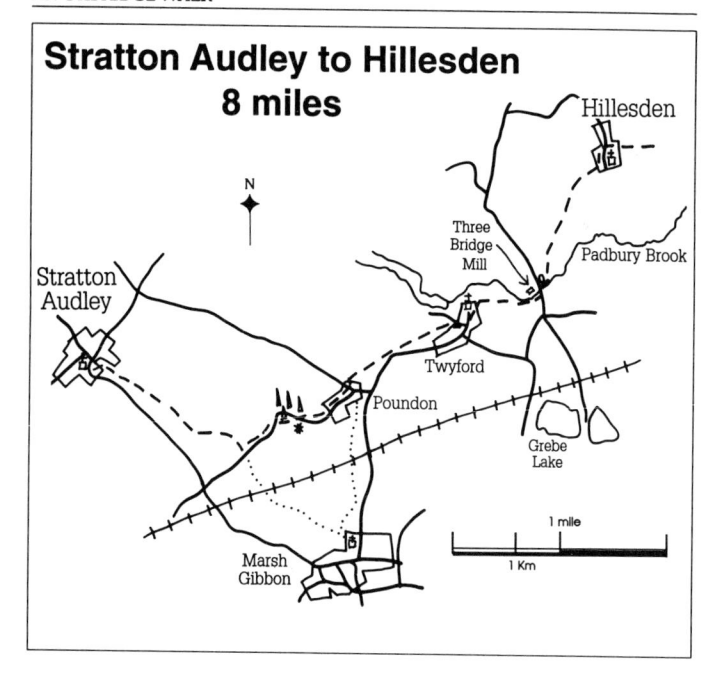

Here, the route turns left for about a mile up Poundon Hill at the top of which the road turns right and runs down into the village of Poundon.

At this point the Oxbridge route takes a short-cut by turning left along the road. The Cross Bucks Way carries on ahead over several more miles of way-marked path across unremarkable, arable farmland, before dipping down to Marsh Gibbon, and then back up again to Poundon.

The route follows the road up Poundon Hill and, just before the top is reached, turns right on a public footpath to follow the chain-link fence on the perimeter of a wireless station. When this fence turns sharply left, the path crosses the gap and keeps to the right of a wooden fence which eventually turns left to a wooden gate.

There are fine views to the south as far as the Chilterns, whilst closer to hand can be seen the group of old brickworks chimneys once operated by the London Brick Company. The huge, worked out pits of Oxford clay have been partly infilled and/or allowed to fill with water to form the Calvert Jubilee nature reserve managed by BBONT.

From the gate, the path goes ahead over a short pasture to re-join the road, where the route turns right. After a short distance downhill the imposing neo-Georgian frontage of Poundon House is passed on the right, next door to Manor Farm (B+B accommodation available). A few hundred yards further on, the T junction in the centre of the village is reached, with the Sow and Pigs pub on the right.

The route turns left at the T junction and, after a few yards, right where a way-marked stile next to the gates to a small Anglian Water depot indicates the continuation of the Cross Bucks Way. From here the path follows the hedge-line and, after about a hundred yards, switches to the other side of the hedge via a stile. It then runs diagonally left, across a field, then over a double stile and footbridge from where the path bears to the right across a wide pasture, aiming to the left of the grey farm buildings of Red Furlong Farm. In the top right-hand corner of this field, stiles take the route across a farm-road followed by a wide pasture, aiming for the right-hand of the four ash trees close together in the hedge on the far side. From here the path clips the corner of the next field to a double stile and footbridge through the hedge to the left of the barn. The path now leads across a wide, arable field, heading just to the right of the squat tower of Twyford church seen ahead in the middle distance. On the other side of this field, the path crosses a small pasture and then runs through a farmyard, on the other side of which the route turns left along a lane.

Turn right for Twyford village shop and The Crown - B+B accommodation available.

The route follows the lane and forks right along School Lane, at the end of which the Cross Bucks Way is way-marked over a stile on a path leading past the village church.

Twyford parish church is dedicated to the Assumption of St Mary and has a main structure dating from the fourteenth and fifteenth centuries with some features of an earlier date. The door is fifteenth century and still operates smoothly on its original hinges. Inside there are many interesting

Three Bridge Mill

features and ornate memorials. Close by the church is the old vicarage, now privately owned, built on the site of an early monastery.

Just past the church, the path crosses the dismantled Great Central Railway line, on the other side of which it turns right along the fence for about 50 yards and then left, keeping to the left of the first hedge. At the end of the hedge-line, the path continues in the same direction across a pasture and then over a footbridge. From here, it bears right across a small pasture bordering a mill-stream along which it turns right to Three Bridge Mill.

A water-powered mill has stood on this site since at least the eleventh century.

The path turns sharply left, across the mill-stream immediately in front of the mill, and then turns right on a track between the mill-pond and a small factory. At the T junction, the route crosses the track to turn left, behind the hedge, and then right at a way-marked oak-post after which it meets the main road.

At the T junction after the mill, the track to the right leads to the nearby Seven Stars pub, the last chance for refreshments for the next 7 miles or so.

The route crosses straight over the road and through large, black metal gates to run along the right-hand side of Jubilee Lake. Past the lake, the path crosses a wide, arable field, aiming to the right of a group of evergreens in the hedgerow on the far side. From here it keeps ahead across two more arable fields, aiming for the tower of Hillesden church in the middle distance. It then continues to the right hand corner of a third field, from where it follows the line of the hedge before turning right over a stile and then diagonally left, aiming for a gap in the hedge on the other side of a sandy track. The path then continues diagonally right down to a footbridge over a stream after which the path runs up the hill in front directly in line with the tower of Hillesden church sited on the hill-top.

All Saints, the finest Perpendicular church in the county and widely known as the "Cathedral in the Fields", was largely rebuilt on its original twelfth-century foundations by the monks of Notley Abbey (see main Oxbridge route, after Long Crendon). During the Civil War, together with the original Hillesden House then situated next to it, the church held out for the Royalist forces of Charles I whose headquarters was based at Oxford. Twice besieged, it eventually fell to the victorious Parliamentary forces commanded by, amongst others, Colonel Oliver Cromwell. In revenge for its prolonged opposition, Hillesden House was totally destroyed and much damage was inflicted on the church. To this day musket ball holes can still be seen in the door of the north porch.)

There are no refreshments or B+B available in Hillsden.

HILLESDEN - ADDINGTON - WINSLOW - SWANBOURNE
(9 miles)

Of particular interest

Addington, barn and stocks; Winslow market town and Winslow Hall; Swanbourne church (plaque in chancel floor).

From here the route leads through the large, ornamental gates in front of the church and follows an avenue lined with young horse chestnut trees for about a mile. At the end of the avenue, the path turns sharply left, then over a stile and right along a bridleway. The path runs for a short distance before crossing over Padbury Brook,

AN OXBRIDGE WALK

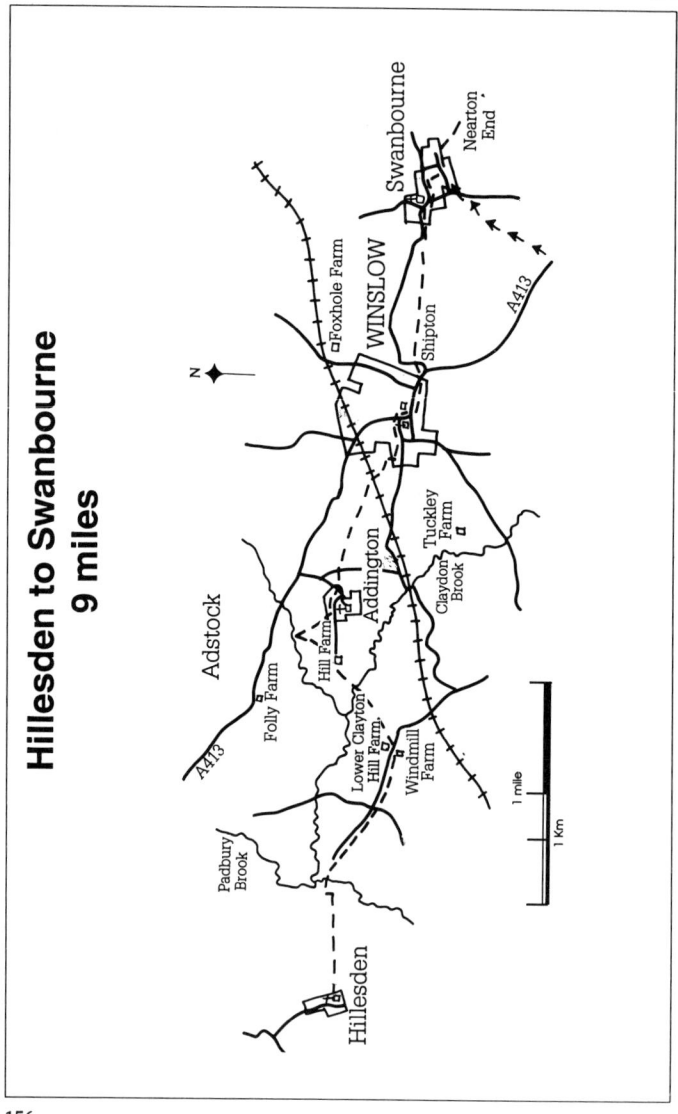

via Kings Bridge, and continues ahead to eventually become a metalled lane when it reaches Lower Kingsbridge Farm.

From here, the Cross Bucks Way follows the lane up to and straight over a crossroads after which it follows the road for about half a mile. Just after passing Windmill Hill Farm on the right, the path leaves the road on the left, at a way-marked stile to the right of some roadside barns belonging to Claydon Hill Farm. From the road, the path heads diagonally right, crossing under a line of pylons, and then continues ahead over the dismantled Buckingham to Aylesbury railway line. From here the path keeps ahead and then angles to the left of a small poplar wood, where it crosses a footbridge over Claydon Brook, one of the early tributaries of the river Great Ouse.

The path continues in the same direction under a second line of electricity pylons and then up the rise towards the rear of Hill Farm. A grey metal gate on the right takes the path across a short pasture to a stile each side of a farm-track. From here it carries on diagonally right up and across the top of the rise, over another stile and through a gateway. From here it crosses a wide pasture, aiming for the left of three dead trees, to the far side of the field.

Having arrived at the footbridge and stile on the far side of the field, those looking for B+B at Folly Farm, or refreshments in the village of Adstock, should carry on along this field path and turn left where it meets the road. Also, at this point, due to the restrictions imposed by existing rights-of-way, the Cross Bucks Way virtually doubles back on itself, ie. having walked as far as this stile in a north-easterly direction, the route almost doubles back on itself in a south-easterly direction.

From this side of the footbridge and stile, the route almost does an about turn (if in doubt check the direction in which the finger-post is pointing), and manages to leave via a double stile and footbridge, half-way down on what is now the left-hand side of the field. From here the path crosses an arable field after which the route turns left on a lane for a short distance into the hamlet of Addington.

Addington has some interesting buildings, including the oldest cruciform barn in the county, one of a cluster of substantial farm buildings passed on the right and in front of which the old village stocks have been re-sited. There are some impressive buildings in Addington but, judging by the number of prominently displayed "Strictly Private" signs, Addington is seriously concerned to maintain its obvious exclusivity. The church of St Mary the Virgin contains interesting memorials including one to a past headmaster of Westminster School who declined to doff his cap to Charles II in case the boys thought that someone was more important than the master... The church has some fine Netherlandish glass and a comprehensive guide to Addington for those who may wish to discover more about its history and buildings.

Past the farm buildings on the right, the route continues ahead at a junction (turn right if visiting the church). After a few hundred yards it continues ahead, past the gates to Addington Manor (where the North Bucks Way, which has kept the route company since Addington church, turns left along the road), and eventually meets the road where it turns right. About 50 yards along the road, the route turns left over a way-marked stile next to a white, metal gate.

From here a path heads diagonally right, down across a long pasture, clipping the corner of a small wood from where it carries on to a footbridge and stile in the bottom right-hand corner. It then continues in the same direction across a long, arable field, heading again for a stile in the far right hand corner. From here it travels about 50 yards past the end of a small wood and turns right over another stile. The path then crosses diagonally left across a sloping pasture and over a stile in the hedge, from where it continues down to and across the Oxford to Bletchley railway line.

This line has not carried passengers for some years and is currently under notice of complete closure. Once dismantled, only the road bridges and embankment will survive to mark the course of what was once a direct rail-link between Oxford and Cambridge.

On the other side of the railway line, the path continues ahead over stiles each side of a narrow pasture. It then leads diagonally left over two more stiles and pastures, after which it meets a narrow lane. Straight over the lane, the route follows a chain link fence around the perimeter of a small school. At the end of the fence, it turns left along the backs of some houses and over stile. From here it follows the path which bends right at the end of the houses and down to the road. Here the route turns left along the road and continues ahead until a T junction in the centre of the town where it turns right down to the market square.

Winslow has been a market town since at least the thirteenth century. Its

Winslow Hall

attractive market square is surrounded by eighteenth- and nineteenth-century houses, shops and inns, including The George, which has a wrought iron balcony brought from nearby Claydon House (National Trust), and the handsome, columned door and bay windows of The Bell (B+B accommodation available). Just off the square, the church of St Laurence is noted for its fifteenth century wall paintings, one of which depicts the murder of Thomas Beckett. The Baptist Church, dating from 1695, is probably the oldest non-conformist place of worship in the county.

From the bottom of the market square the Cross Bucks Way turns left along the A413, signposted to Aylesbury, and after a few hundred yards passes Winslow Hall.

Winslow Hall was built between 1698 and 1702, almost certainly to designs by Sir Christopher Wren, for William Lowndes, Secretary of the Treasury during Queen Anne's reign. The house is tall, of red and grey brick with stone dressings. Inside, the house has an impressive collection of eighteenth-century furniture and fine pictures, whilst the grounds contain some rarities that will interest keen gardeners. The house and gardens are open to the public on some afternoons in the summer months of July and August. For further information tel (01296) 712323.

The route continues to follow the road ahead, ignoring the first left hand lane opposite the school. Further on, where the road bends right, it turns left up Shipton Lane (B4032). At the second left-hand bend, just past the farm buildings on the right, the Cross Bucks Way is signposted along a track to the right. From a gateway next to a large ash tree, the path continues more or less ahead, across an arable field to a stile in the hedge on the right. From here the path clips the corner of the next field to another stile after which it turns right to follow the hedge-line. Eventually, it turns right through a gap in the hedge and heads down across another arable field to a double stile and substantial footbridge. From here, it keeps ahead to the corner of a small pasture and then continues down a long field, keeping to the right of a line of electricity poles, to where it meets the road.

The route turns right along the road into the village of Swanbourne, on the outskirts of which it briefly joins the Swans/Midshires Way as it passes the only roadside tea rooms since leaving Oxford. At the T junction next to the church, the route turns left.

Swanbourne's church has an unusual plaque set in the chancel floor which commemorates Robert Adams who, on 17th October 1626, "In prime of youth by bloudy thieves was slaine" The plaque depicts Robert Adams, his wife and four children. To the west of the church, and visible from the road, is a fine Tudor Manor House built as the home of Sir John Fortescue, cousin of Queen Elizabeth I. Royalist troops burnt down part of the village in the Civil War, however, a good number of buildings survived, including Deverell's Farm, another stone house with mullioned windows and dated 1632.

Today, Swanbourne, like so many other villages, shows more the ill-effects of total reliance on the motor car than any depredations caused by war. The village had its own station, but the last train ran in 1967. Once virtually self-sufficient, the last pub has closed and the village bakery has been turned into a tea rooms. Close to the tea rooms stands a tiny building which, prewar, was the village cobblers, and which itself stood next to the smithy, now long gone - village lore has it that the same man ran both, and that he could put a sole on your shoe at the same time as he put a shoe on your horse!

Having turned left at the T junction, the route follows the road past Deverell's Farm and then the post office/shop on the left, to turn right at a way-marked finger-post to the left of Old House. From here a metalled path runs downhill at the bottom of which it meets the lane in Nearton End, where the main, southerly route of the Oxbridge Walk comes in from the right.

From this point on, there is only one route to Cambridge, described in the section headed "Swanbourne to Leighton Buzzard".

ALTERNATIVE ROUTE - GENERAL INFORMATION - BUCKINGHAMSHIRE

En Route

Of particular interest	Poundon - Beacon Hill - views
	Twyford church
	Three Bridge Mill
	Hillesden church
	Addington, barn and stocks
	Winslow - Winslow Hall
	Swanbourne church
Accommodation	Poundon - Manor Farm (01869) 277212
	Twyford - Crown Inn (01296) 730216
	Nr. Padbury - Folly Farm (01296) 712413
	Winslow - Tuckey Farm (01296) 713208
	- The Bell Hotel (01296) 714091
	- Foxhole Farm, (Little Horwood Rd) (01296) 714550
Refreshments	Poundon - one pub
	Twyford - one pub
	Three Bridge Mill - one pub
	Winslow - restaurants, pubs, cafes
PO/shops	Twyford - small supermarket
	Winslow - PO, mini-markets
Public phone	Poundon, Twyford,
	Hillesden, Addington, Winslow
Banks	Winslow only
Parking	Roadside only
	Winslow - free car park
Misc	Winslow - market day Wed
Access to Winslow	Road A413 between Buckingham and Aylesbury
	Rail Nearest Station, Bletchley (Milton Keynes) (01908) 370883
	Bus (01296) 84919
For Swanbourne	(see main route)

Appendix

Official, Way-marked, Middle- and Long-distance Footpaths in the Four Counties Traversed by the Oxbridge Route

OXFORDSHIRE

11 circular walks and 4 circular rides.

The Oxfordshire Way	65 miles from Bourton-on-the-Water, Gloucs, to Henley-on-Thames
The Ridgeway	85 miles from Ivinghoe Beacon, Bucks, to Avebury, Wilts
The Thames Walk	156 miles from the source of the Thames, Gloucs, to London. (Planned official launch, 1995)
D'Arcy Dalton Way	65 miles from Wormleighton Reservoir on the Oxford Canal, to Wayland's Smithy on the Ridgeway Path
Thame Valley Walk	See below

BUCKINGHAMSHIRE

20 circular walks, 4 circular rides.

Cross Bucks Way	24 miles linking with the North Bucks/Midshires/Swan's Way and the Greensand Ridge Walk in Bedfordshire
North Bucks Way	35 miles, from the Ridgeway in the Chilterns near Wendover and connects with the Grafton Way near Wolverton
South Bucks Way	23 miles, from the Ridgeway at Coombe Hill near Wendover to Denham and the Grand Union Canal near Hillingdon
The Chess Valley Walk	10 miles along the River Chess (Connects with 4 London Transport tube stations)

The Beeches Way	16 miles, connects the River Thames near Cookham to the Grand Union Canal at West Drayton
Two Ridges Link	8 miles connecting the Ridgeway at Ivinghoe with the Greensand Ridge Walk near Leighton Buzzard
Chiltern Link	8 miles from Wendover to Chesham linking the Ridgeway with the Chess Valley Walk
Aylesbury Ring Walk	31 miles, in the Vale of Aylesbury
Aylesbury Arm	6 miles from Aylesbury to Marsworth Junction, to link with Grand Union Canal Walk
The Swans Way	65 miles, bridleway from Goring-on-Thames to Salcey Forest
The Midshires Way	225 miles, linking the Ridgway in the south with the Trans-Pennine Trail and the Pennine Way in the north
The Three Shires	37 miles, bridle-way from Tathall End, Bucks, to Grafham Water, Cambs
Thame Valley Walk	15 miles, from Albury, Oxon, to Aylesbury, linking Oxfordshire Way, North Bucks/Midshires Way and Swan's Way
Grand Union Canal	145 miles, from Little Venice in London to Gas Street Basin in Birmingham
The Ridgeway	See above
Milton Keynes Boundary Walk	60 mile circular walk

BEDFORDSHIRE

14 circular walks.

Greensand Ridge Walk	42 miles from Leighton Buzzard to Gamlingay Cinques (Cambs)
Lea Valley Walk	50 miles, from London to Luton
Icknield Way	120 miles, from Ivinghoe Beacon, Beds, to Knettishall Heath, Suffolk. (Connects the Ridgeway with the Peddars Way.) Walkers' and riders' routes available
Three Shires Way	See above

AN OXBRIDGE WALK

Grand Union Canal Walk	See above
Two Ridges Link	See above

CAMBRIDGESHIRE

10 walks, including circular walks, 1 circular ride.

The Clopton Way	11 miles from Gamlingay to Wimpole (connects with Wimpole Way)
The Wimpole Way	11 miles from Wimpole Hall to Cambridge
The Ouse Valley Way	25 miles from Bluntisham to Eaton Socon
Nene Way	10 miles in Cambs from Wansford Railway Station to Peterborough
The Hereward Way	110 miles from Oakham Railway Station, Leics, to Thetford, Suffolk. (Links Viking Way with Peddars Way)
Icknield Way	See above
Three Shires Way	See above

APPENDIX

Some Useful Addresses

ADDRESSES FOR WAY-MARKING ETC. ON THE OXBRIDGE ROUTE - SEE INTRODUCTION

Backpackers Club, PO Box 381, Reading, Berks RG3 4RL. (01491) 628739

BBONT (Berks Bucks and Oxon Naturalists Trust), 3 Church Cowley Rd, Rose Hill, Oxford OX4 3JR. (01865) 775476

British Waterways, Willow Grange, Church Rd, Watford, Herts WD1 3QA. (01923) 226422

Camping and Caravanning Club Ltd, Greenfields House, Westwood Way, Coventry CV4 8JH. (01203) 694995

Council for the Protection of Rural England (CPRE), Warwick House, 25 Buckingham Palace Rd, London SW1W OPP. (0171) 976 6433

Countryside Commission, John Dower House, Crescent Place, Cheltenham, Gloucs GL50 3RA. (01242) 521381

English Heritage, Keysign House, 429 Oxford Street, London W1R 2HD. (0171) 973 3457

English Nature (Nature Conservancy Council for England), Northminster House, Northminster Rd, Peterborough PE1 1UA. (01733) 340345

English Tourist Board, Thames Tower, Blacks Rd, Hammersmith, London W6 9EL.

Forestry Commission, 231 Corstophine Rd, Edinburgh EH12 7AT. (0131) 334 0303

Landmark Trust, Shottesbrooke, Maidenhead, Berks SL6 3SW. (01628) 825925

Long Distance Paths Advisory Service Ltd, c/o Peter Robins, 11 Cotswold Court, Sandy Lane, Chester CH3 5U2. (01244) 316517

Long Distance Walkers Association, c/o Kevin Uzzell, 7 Ford Drive, Yarnfield, Stone, Staffs, ST15 ORP. (01785) 760684

Maps   HMSO, 49 High Holborn, London WC1V 6HB. (0171) 873 0011

        Maps by Mail, PO Box 350A, Surbiton, Surrey KT5 9LX. (0181) 399 4970

        Stanfords, 12-14 Long Acre, Covent Garden, London WC2E 9LP. (0171) 836 1321

National Trust, 36 Queen Anne's Gate, London SW1H 9AS.
(0171) 222 9251

Ordnance Survey, Romsey Rd, Maybush, Southampton, Hants SO9 4DH.
(01703) 792000

Ramblers' Association, 1-5 Wandsworth Rd, London SW8 2XX.
(0171) 582 6878

Royal Society for the Protection of Birds, (RSPB), The Lodge, Sandy, Beds SG19 2DL. (01767) 680551

Tourist Information Offices, (Oxford and Cambridge) - See Introduction.

Wildlife Trust:

Beds - Priory Country Park, Barkers Lane, Bedford MK41 9SH. (01234) 364213

Cambs - Enterprise House, Maris Lane, Trumpington, Cambridge CB2 2LE. (01223) 846363

Youth Hostels Association (YHA), Trevelyan House, 8 St Stephen's Hill, St Albans, Herts AL1 2DY. (01727) 55215

CICERONE GUIDEBOOKS

Cicerone produce an unrivalled selection of reliable guide books for outdoor enthusiasts. Many of the books provide inspiration for memorable holidays or day outings. The guides are practical and pocket sized.
Areas covered include Britain, Europe and many other interesting locations worldwide.

WALKING IN THE CHILTERNS
Duncan Unsworth
35 short circular walks in this lovely area of woods and little valleys, with cosy pubs and old churches. The routes are mainly half-day or gentle full-day outings, designed to take in the best of the Chiltern landscape and to visit historical curiosities.
184pp includes many colour and black and white photos, and route maps. £6.99 plus postage.

Available from most bookshops, most outdoor equipment shops, or direct from the publishers
CICERONE PRESS, 2 Police Square, Milnthorpe, Cumbria, LA7 7PY

High

mountain / sports **incorporating 'Mountain INFO'**

Britain's liveliest and most authorative magazine for mountaineers, climbers and ambitious hillwalkers. Gives news and commentary from the UK and worldwide, backed up by exciting features and superb colour photography.

OFFICIAL MAGAZINE

Have you read it yet?

Available monthly from your newsagent or specialist gear shop.

Call 0533 460722 for details

BRITISH MOUNTAINEERING COUNCIL

OUTDOORS
ILLUSTRATED

The leading all-outdoor magazine covering the active outdoors in Britain and abroad. Climbing, hiking, trekking, sailing, skiing, canoeing, diving, paragliding, travel and more. Regular features on health, equipment, photography, wildlife and environment. All in full colour throughout.

QUARTERLY from leading newsagents

Studio 2, 114-116 Walcot Street, Bath BA1 5BG

IF YOU LIKE ADVENTUROUS ACTIVITIES ON MOUNTAINS OR HILLS YOU WILL ENJOY

CLIMBER

& *HILLWALKER*

**MOUNTAINEERING/HILLWALKING/TREKKING
ROCK CLIMBING/SCRAMBLING IN BRITAIN
AND ABROAD**

*AVAILABLE FROM NEWSAGENTS, OUTDOOR EQUIPMENT SHOPS,
OR BY SUBSCRIPTION (6-12 MONTHS) FROM
CALEDONIAN MAGAZINES LTD, PLAZA TOWER,
EAST KILBRIDE, GLASGOW G74 1LW*

THE WALKERS' MAGAZINE

TGO
THE GREAT OUTDOORS

**COMPULSIVE MONTHLY READING FOR
ANYONE INTERESTED IN WALKING**

*AVAILABLE FROM NEWSAGENTS, OUTDOOR EQUIPMENT SHOPS,
OR BY SUBSCRIPTION (6-12 MONTHS) FROM
CALEDONIAN MAGAZINES LTD, PLAZA TOWER,
EAST KILBRIDE, GLASGOW G74 1LW*